SPREADING
JOY

SPREADING
JOY

How Joyalukkas Became
the World's Favourite Jeweller

JOY ALUKKAS

WITH THOMAS SCARIA AND NIDHI JAIN

HARPER
BUSINESS

An Imprint of HarperCollins *Publishers*

First published in India by Harper Business 2023
An imprint of HarperCollins *Publishers*
4th Floor, Tower A, Building No. 10, DLF Cyber City,
DLF Phase II, Gurugram, Haryana – 122002
www.harpercollins.co.in

2 4 6 8 10 9 7 5 3

P-ISBN: 978-93-5699-526-0
E-ISBN: 978-93-5699-527-7

Typeset in 11.5/16 ITC Galliard at
Manipal Technologies Limited, Manipal

Printed and bound at
Thomson Press (India) Ltd.

To Appan and Amma, who somehow taught me everything
I know, without ever telling me what to do

Contents

Prologue

━⟨✦⟩━

The car salesman looked down his long nose at me, gaze flickering contemptuously over my modest attire, and inquired tersely, 'What do you want?'

I gestured at the magnificent Rolls Royce Silver Seraph seductively displayed on a ramp to his left.

'I want to see this car,' I replied.

He sneered, and said derisively, 'This car is not for viewing. It is for sale, and it is very, very expensive.'

The salesman, possibly of Levantine ethnicity, had taken exception to my Indian identity, and apparent lack of resources. In Dubai, nothing speaks louder than the dirham, and in 2001, Indian expatriates in the Gulf were not regarded as a prosperous community. As far as he was concerned, I was riffraff, sullying the hallowed ground of the Rolls Royce showroom.

Had he known that I could have gold-plated his Rolls Royce, he would doubtless have rolled out the red carpet.

But, having jumped to the conclusion that I was just another hick who had wandered in to gawk at a luxury car, he pointed peremptorily to the neighbouring showroom, which was devoted to Mitsubishi automobiles, saying, 'You want car, you go there.' Then he turned away, as if I were unworthy of notice.

I felt a stirring of rage, as much on my own behalf as that of my countrymen who, in those days, tended to suffer disrespect more often than not. My unassuming demeanour had led the salesman to believe he could get away with cheeky behaviour.

My presence in the showroom was incidental. I had dropped in at Al Habtoor Motors to meet my friend Ashraf, who was Mitsubishi's regional sales head. They were dealers for Rolls Royce as well. Ashraf had stepped out of his office, and while waiting for him, I spotted the Silver Seraph in the adjacent showroom and walked over to get a closer look at it. That's when the salesman accosted me, and made me the object of his gratuitous discourtesy.

At that moment, Ashraf and the company's chief financial officer walked in. As soon as we had exchanged greetings, I announced that I was going to buy the Rolls Royce. Suddenly, I was the object of the entire showroom's attention.

'That car?' one of them asked, pointing at the ramp.

'Yes,' I said firmly.

'But that's only for display. If you place an order, we will get you a new car.'

'No, I want this one.'

I was well aware that purchasing a display piece was unheard of, because Rolls Royce required prior booking. But I dug in my heels.

'This is the one I want. And I want it now.'

A stunned silence followed. They realized that I was dead serious. Then, the paperwork commenced; I paid on the spot, and returned to the office with my prize.

Now came the one-million-dirham question: what was I to do with it?

I had acted on impulse. My decision to buy the car had been purely emotional, but now, the rational part of my brain kicked in. I had an epiphany—in a single stroke, I could turn the whole incident to my advantage, and send Rolls Royce a salutary message at the same time.

Sales promotions often involved automobiles. Customers love freebies, and offering up middle-range cars in lucky draws was a cost-effective way of boosting sales. Our advertisement announced that a customer who purchased five hundred dirhams worth of jewellery would be entitled to a raffle coupon, and would get a chance to win … hold your breath … a Rolls Royce!

Designed by the prominent ad agency Madco Gulf, it featured a tower of gold bangles topped by the trademark 'Spirit of Ecstasy' hood ornament. Below it was a picture of the Silver Seraph itself—a symphony of sensuous lines, gleaming exterior and chrome trim, with a number plate proclaiming 'RR 1'. The ad invited customers to 'win the world's No. 1 car' from the 'world's No. 1 22-karat jeweller'.

The impact was beyond what I had imagined. The city was agog. Never had a top-end luxury car been given away by a retailer. It became a talking point, and customers streamed in. Some bought jewellery; others just wanted to buy a coupon! All at once, the Alukkas jewellery brand had been catapulted to another level.

The subliminal association between Alukkas and a high-end luxury automobile brand boosted our standing. It was a win-win. I had made my point, and Alukkas had marked its presence in the United Arab Emirates with a bang. Thereafter, Rolls Royce decided that their cars would no longer figure in raffle promotions. Even the Dubai airport duty-free retail, which featured Rolls Royce cars in its promotional campaigns, was asked not to do so.

For me, the episode was a vindication: I had spent too many years as the family underdog to lightly accept intimidation in any shape or form.

1

A Diamond in the Rough

‹ Joy has no head for business.'

My brothers said it so often and with such conviction that it became a byword in the Alukkas family. Business-oriented as we were, this was seen as a major flaw in my character.

The signature family business was a jewellery store. It was manned by my older brothers and I rarely showed up there. My mother perpetually complained and my sisters echoed, 'He is never in the shop! He cycles around all day, doing nothing!'

If my siblings had been asked which of the five Alukkas brothers was most likely to succeed in business, I would have been at the bottom of the ranking. Decades later, after I made it to the Forbes' list of billionaires, my sister Clara would say, 'Seeing Joy as a child and watching him grow up, I never thought he would be a big success.'

For as long as I can remember, I had attracted censure for gallivanting around the town instead of helping out in our shops.

My numerous failings and my refusal to conform were a frequent topic of discussion among my siblings. I was—they believed—financially illiterate. Numbers defined our livelihood, and my alleged disinterest in keeping accounts implied that I was fit for none but the most menial jobs, such as running domestic or business-related errands, or acting as my father's gofer.

My father (or Appan as we called him), a stern and taciturn patriarch noted for his entrepreneurial skills, never commented on my abilities, or lack thereof. He, of all my family members, must have known that I was not a shirker; I had dogged his footsteps from boyhood up and cast myself in the role of his man Friday. In the process, I absorbed by osmosis the minutiae of the various businesses that he ran.

I was up to all the tasks he set me. What's more, I anticipated his needs and did whatever was required, even without being told. I was able to see things the way he did, with the same sharp eye for detail.

As a child, I had got into the habit of keeping meticulous accounts of my own expenses. This came in handy when Appan began assigning odd jobs to me. True, I never sat in the showroom, but I did everything he asked of me with diligence, while applying my own mind to the task.

My father was the centre of my world. He was my captain. To him, I gave complete and absolute obedience. I regarded myself as his servitor and devoted all my energies to his comforts, big and small. I was always there to open the door of his car, to drive him if the chauffeur failed to showed up, or to orchestrate men and materials for his construction projects.

I loved being his assistant. I had learnt to ride a motorcycle at the age of fourteen, and was driving cars by the time I was sixteen. This mobility allowed me to run countless errands for him, and had the added advantage of keeping me at arm's length from my demanding brothers. Besides, I enjoyed dealing with people from different walks of life. I am convinced that, on any given day, I learned far more about the world of business as Appan's side than my brothers did in the showroom.

What could be duller and more restrictive than sitting at a cash counter or serving customers? In my view, these were jobs for employees, whereas a true entrepreneur took a more holistic approach to his enterprise. I was not as clueless about the business as my brothers supposed. I understood sales and margins, but held my peace and concentrated on doing whatever my father required of me.

Appan rarely came to my defence when my brothers made disparaging remarks. On the other hand, he never judged me. The very fact that he entrusted me with challenging tasks argued that I had earned his confidence (or so I believed) and that was enough for me. I did not need to prove my worth to anyone else. I was resilient and could take slights in my stride.

The Alukkas showroom was my father's second such venture—our first jewellery store had opened in Thrissur in 1956, the year I was born. It sold gold and silver trinkets, and like most jewellers at the time, offered nose and earlobe-piercing. The store was not particularly successful and in 1959, my father shut shop.

Appan pragmatically chose to close the business rather than incur losses. At the time, downing shutters on an enterprise took courage, because it was seen as an admission of failure, and was usually followed by social disapprobation. When I heard the story, it spoke of my father's sound business sense. 'Never hold on to a dead horse; it can prove very expensive,' he would say. I have always followed that advice.

Appan exited the gold business and concentrated on his other existing ventures: textile printing and umbrella manufacturing. A stationery shop, a radio agency and businesses in real estate and hospitality were to follow later.

Shutting the jewellery shop did not dampen his spirit. Nor did it mean that he lost interest in the jewellery industry; indeed, he closely followed developments in the sector. The Gold Control Act was passed in 1962, under the aegis of then finance minister, Morarji Desai. Stringent in the extreme, the act recalled all the gold loans given by banks, and banned forward trading in gold. In 1963, the manufacture of gold jewellery above 14-karat purity was proscribed. It came as a crushing blow for retailers, because Indian jewellery was traditionally made of 22-karat gold. Buyers began purchasing directly from goldsmiths, and intermediaries were squeezed out of the market.

Seeking Their Fortune

Born Puthussery Alukka Joseph Varghese in 1913, my father was originally from Angamaly, where my paternal grandfather, Puthussery Alukka Joseph had been an agriculturist. My grandparents had a large family, as was the norm in those days, and the income from farming was insufficient to sustain them all. In the 1930s, my grandfather moved his family to Thrissur (then called Trichur) in search of opportunities. Situated some fifty kilometres from Angamaly, it was a flourishing hub of trade and industry, where employment was easily available.

The Syrian Christian community, to which Appan belonged, was not unaccustomed to migration. They had moved en masse from Kottayam to the Malabar region in the early twentieth century, a trend that continued right up to the 1980s. Legend has it that the history of the community goes back two millennia, to the advent of St. Thomas the Apostle in Kerala. He is believed to have landed at Kodungallur near Cochin (now Kochi) in 52 CE, and established seven churches before he passed away in Mylapore two decades later. The appellation 'Syrian' owes to the Syriac liturgical practices that the church follows.

The community enjoys a high social standing, and took the lead in modern education and economic activities as early as the nineteenth century. Today, it has evolved into a community of agriculturists, scholars, industrialists and professionals.

Thrissur, the gold capital of Kerala, was noted for a culture of entrepreneurship. Jewellery and banking emerged as core sectors, and the town attracted significant investment. It was a hub of jewellery manufacturing, with some 3,000 units employing thousands of artisans, and turned out 70 per cent of the gold jewellery in the state. To this day, the quality of Thrissur's craftsmanship is famous among Indians across the world.

The west coast of the subcontinent, between the Western Ghats and the Arabian Sea, had been a repository of gold for millennia, received in exchange for spices and textiles. Indeed, it is said to have drained dry the coffers of the Roman empire. The town of Thrissur came into prominence in the seventeenth century, when Sakthan Thampuran, the ruler of Cochin, shifted his residential palace there. It was he who introduced Thrissur Pooram, a landmark seven-day cultural festival in honour of the Hindu God, Shiva, celebrated to this day.

At the time, Thrissur's professional demography comprised traders, businessmen and courtiers with large houses in streets, some of which are still in existence. The district had long been a melting pot of different cultures and religions, resulting in an inclusive spirit—it was at the forefront of a nationwide movement to abolish untouchability—which further contributed to the business ethos.

Appan was in his early twenties when my grandfather passed away. As the eldest, he took upon himself the responsibility of maintaining the family. His formal education had stopped after the sixth standard, but his business instincts were sharp and by the dint of shrewd trading, he managed to support the clan. From my older siblings, I gathered that his activities ranged from selling earthen pots at the Wednesday market to working at Chakolas Textiles.

His big break was owed to an accident at sea. He was working at Chakolas Textiles when he heard that a ship carrying a large consignment of milled cloth had sunk. The shipment of cloth was rescued and it arrived at Cochin. The owner told Appan he could take it all, free of cost, as it was no longer of any use to him.

My father gratefully accepted it, and was pleasantly surprised to discover that the cloth was in good shape. He used it to begin a textile-printing business out of a shed in the compound of the family house, which was surrounded by around half an acre of land, the minimum that almost every family owned in those days. He produced white dhotis with printed borders—standard menswear in those days. Printing was done manually and was a laborious process, involving the use of dyes, moulds and seals. Later, he expanded his operations to include coloured textiles.

He always had his ear to the ground, and a penchant for spotting opportunities. When packing materials were in demand, he set up a manufacturing line. Another time, when cement was in short supply, he purchased wholesale bags and repackaged them in lots of one to five kilo bags for resale. He made a decent profit and exited the business as soon as the shortage ended.

My sister, Mary, the third of my parents' offspring, recalls that Appan was fascinated by building and construction. Sundays would find him at the Peechi or Idukki Dam construction sites. That passion was to draw him into real estate. Alongside his other ventures, he began buying and selling land and buildings.

My father also entered umbrella trade, courtesy a former employee of Chakolas Textiles, who had started an umbrella unit and wanted him to handle the distribution. Eventually, Appan got into manufacturing for himself, and succeeded far beyond his expectations. Starting out with twenty-five workers, he set up the unit in the shed at our home. It was a conscious decision, because a home-based cottage industry was less open to labour unionism.

From the 1940s onwards, a powerful Left movement swept the region that was to become Kerala, and in 1957, the new state's very first election brought in a Communist regime. Trade unions mushroomed all over the province, and their fierce advocacy of labour rights became a challenge for entrepreneurs. The rise of trade unionism in Kerala impacted industries in the state, with the result that many of them shifted out to greener pastures. Thrissur, once an important hub for cutting and polishing diamonds, lost out to Surat in Gujarat, which quickly became the diamond capital of India. But banking and jewellery continued to thrive in Thrissur.

The umbrella business was our mainstay throughout the early 1960s. Our schools were chosen for their proximity to the umbrella factory which, by then, had a workforce of a hundred. I had started my education at St. Joseph School Church in 1962, but was shifted to St. Thomas High School with the rest of my male siblings, because it was closer to my father's place of work.

In tandem with Appan's businesses, the family expanded. Rooms were added to the house as the numbers increased year by year. Even so, there was a perpetual space crunch. My parents, Varghese and Eliya, had married young, and large families were de rigueur in those days. Their marriage was arranged, in keeping with the tradition among conservative Syrian Christian families.

The Alukka children, in order of chronology, were: Elsi, Jos, Mary, Kochuthresya, Rosily, Lucy, Jacintha, Philomina, Paul, Francis, Joy, Clara, Anto, Reena and Pauly. Thus, I was the eleventh of fifteen siblings.

A Boy with a Difference

My earthly journey almost came to an end as soon as it began, for I was a 'blue baby'. Seconds after I was born at two in the morning on 29 October 1956, I turned cyanotic, a condition caused by low oxygen levels in the blood. So dim were my chances of survival that a 'baptism at home' was held, and I was given a name: Joy.

In the circumstances, the choice of name was certainly counterintuitive. My sister, Jacintha, who told me the story of my birth, maintains the family elders had decided on the felicitous name hoping, perhaps, that it would lend a touch of peace to my brief time on earth.

Call it fate, divine intervention, or sheer blind luck, the obstruction in my airways miraculously cleared, and I began to breathe normally. The blue tint disappeared and I joined the ranks of the Alukka family. My mother never told me any of this; perhaps she wanted to forget how close she had come to losing me. I, naturally, have no memory of my postpartum triumph over death. Yet from boyhood up, I always felt that I was somehow different from all the rest.

In later years, my sisters would say that I had been well-named, because I had a certain joie de vivre. I was known as jovial and naughty, unlike my serious siblings! Incidentally, most of the Alukka children were born at home, with the help of a midwife. Only the last three—Anto, Reena and Pauly— were born in the hospital.

One of my father's defining characteristics was an intolerance of dust, dirt and clutter. Amma (my mother), ever mindful of the maxim 'cleanliness is next to godliness', ensured that the house was swept and swabbed from top to bottom every day, the cobwebs cleared and every piece of furniture and bric-a-brac dusted. Kitchen waste was never allowed to fester. Dishes had to be washed, and toys or laundry cleared away before Appan returned home from work.

One of my earliest memories is watching my mother sweeping the courtyard of our home alongside the two maids who had been hired to assist her. On one occasion, someone had left a scrap of paper on the floor. It caught my father's eye and triggered an explosion of wrath.

Clara, my junior by two years, recalls how our father once spotted her playing with a broom—she was just three at the time—and laughed, saying, 'When she grows up, she will clean the house very well.'

Growing up, I imbibed Appan's penchant for cleanliness. To this day, I insist on a spotless domestic and business environment. The staff at my home and my showrooms is aware that I have a habit of conducting surprise inspections, not just of the premises but of the vicinity. I also insist on good grooming and high standards of personal hygiene for all my employees. There is no room in my life for clutter. If the mind and the soul are to be unsullied, so must our bodies and environs.

My parents were deeply religious and began each day with a visit to the church. Every morning at five, Appan would ring a bell to summon us from the first floor. All the children who were older than five accompanied them, perforce. It was only after they returned from mass that tea would be served. Amma would busy herself in the kitchen, preparing our breakfast. It was a pleasure to watch her at work; her movements were economical, enabling her to multitask and turn out several dishes at the same time. An accomplished cook, she was known for her Kerala-style fish curry. Her chicken and mutton curry, too, were delectable.

Even as she cooked, Amma would hector us to get ready for school. After we had left, she would attend to her many household chores. The older children were assigned to take care of their younger siblings. Despite her heavy workload, Amma was invariably cheerful, except when one of us annoyed her. Then she became a martinet, and punished us with a heavy hand. The hapless victim of her anger then had to endure taunts from the other siblings.

Generally, Amma was buoyant of spirit. She was talkative and jocular, as if to offset my father's habitual solemnity and reticence. When we (siblings) would fight among ourselves, she would play mediator. She would enter into our childish games with enthusiasm, a practice she continued with her grandchildren until she was well into her eighties.

Dinner was a noisy affair; the one meal of the day we all ate together. My father, for reasons best known to him, sat separately and was served last. Consequently, he usually ended up getting the remnants of our meal, like gravy without fish or stew without mutton, but I never once heard him complain.

As children, we were rather scared of him, to the point that when he entered the house, announcing his presence with a cough, we would run away to our respective rooms or contrive to look busy. He showed his softer side only when my cousins visited, which was often. They all loved him dearly.

Often, Appan would bury himself behind a newspaper when he was home. He was an avid reader, always well-informed on current affairs. He thoroughly enjoyed travelling, and would take Amma with him, leaving us in the care of our Ammamma (grandmother). Once, they took a cruise from Cochin to Bombay (now Mumbai).

Like all little boys, I wanted to be like my father. To this end, I invented a game called Little Dad. It involved wearing one of Appan's shirts and strutting around the house, imperiously rapping out commands to my siblings. They certainly didn't respond with the reverence due to a parent, but I thoroughly enjoyed pretending to be my father.

The Three Rs

My father believed that a practical education was far more useful than a formal one. Certainly, one needed the three Rs—reading, (w)riting and (a)rithmetic—but other than that, life itself was the best teacher.

Appan never stopped learning. For him, knowledge was utilitarian, driven by need. For instance, in his fifties, he, along with an associate, took Hindi tuition. It was an eminently pragmatic measure, for they had discovered—during their regular trips to Bombay to source materials for the manufacture of umbrellas—that Hindi was the lingua franca of the suppliers in the metropolis.

Imbibing my father's somewhat casual outlook vis-à-vis formal education, I would skip school at the slightest opportunity. Nor was the atmosphere at home conducive to studying. A plethora of people would constantly throng the premises, and our younger siblings would inevitably create a racket. In the daily melee, it was impossible to concentrate on our studies.

Paul was the most academically gifted among the brothers. The rest of us got by on the strength of Appan's umbrellas— literally speaking. He used the umbrellas he manufactured to good effect throughout our school days. Every year, he would dispense a score or more to our schoolmasters as a goodwill gesture, in the expectation that they would overlook our academic shortcomings.

He would sally forth to school with the umbrellas, to meet one or the other of my teachers. They would exchange pleasantries before Appan would get down to business. He would turn the conversation to the weather, which in Kerala was usually rainy, and segue deftly into the importance of good quality umbrellas.

'Oh, yes. Umbrellas often break or tear,' the teacher would agree.

'Not to worry. Joy, pass your master six umbrellas,' my father would say.

And that was how I, and most of my older brothers, got through school. But not Paul. He breezed through each class without the annual gifting of umbrellas. After graduating from school, he persuaded my father to send him to college. Appan agreed, but added a caveat that Paul could not neglect his duties at the showroom, come what may. As a result, his college education was short-lived.

Appan walked into the showroom one morning and noted Paul's absence. Learning that he was attending classes in college, he looked displeased. On the following day, he paid a visit to the principal of the college.

He requested the principal to summon Paul, who arrived looking rather apprehensive. Appan pointed out that he had acquiesced to Paul's desire to attend college on the condition that he continued to fulfil his duties in the family business. He had failed to do so. Paul protested that he had left the showroom in order to attend classes, but my father was adamant. He reiterated that Paul was free to study and obtain his degree, but not at the cost of the business. He would have to attend to his duties at the showroom, whether or not he had classes.

The principal intervened, saying that Paul could not earn a degree without attending classes. For Paul, it was a catch-22 situation: he couldn't attend his classes if he had to sit in the showroom, and if he didn't attend classes, there was no point in going to college.

In my case, matters were different. Appan didn't interfere with my education (except for the annual gifting of umbrellas), but my own lack of ability and inclination made me an indifferent student. All through primary and middle school, I was always happy to cut classes. Then, one day, soon after I had finished eighth grade, it dawned on me that I was on the cusp of high school, but had learnt very little during my academic career. So, when one of the nuns, or 'sisters', at the church advised my father to send me to boarding school, I was not averse to the idea. Away from the noisy atmosphere of the house, I would be able to study.

The school in question was close to Thrissur, had an excellent reputation and was known for its high academic standards. The language of instruction was Malayalam. I tried very hard to catch up with my class, but it was a lost cause right from the outset. I had wasted too many years playing truant. Even before the examination results were announced, I knew that I would fail. The one useful thing I learnt at boarding school was to wash and iron my clothes. To this day, I do my own laundry, if time permits.

My father received the news of my dismal results with equanimity. Although he would have liked me to pass school, he was satisfied that I had a good grasp of mathematics and an adequate level of literacy. Those were the fundamental skills he demanded: the ability to deal with numbers, and to read and write with clarity.

To this day, I weigh people as my father did—by their abilities and not their degrees. Academic qualifications alone don't impress me, though I appreciate people who earn them. I look for a 'spark'. I want people with out-of-the-box ideas; those who are creative and have a hunger to achieve, rather than those who rest on their academic laurels. Motivation, ambition, intuition, the capacity to learn and the willingness to go the extra mile are important. All my senior managers are selected on this basis.

Nor have I ever lost my zest for learning. Even in my sixties, I can say with confidence that I can learn absolutely anything within a few months, provided I have a good teacher!

2

The Birth of a Brand

A wonderland of bling lies at the heart of Thrissur. Many of the major jewellery showrooms are scattered in and around the city centre, each one ablaze with gold and gems, dazzling visitors with their exquisite displays.

The picture was very different in 1964, the year my father got back into jewellery retail. The Alukka showroom opened on Thrissur's High Road, in premises previously occupied by our radio store. At this point, the store exhibited ornaments only in silver.

The impact of the Gold Control Act of 1962 was being felt. Morarji Desai's restrictions on the gold trade had been envisaged as a means of curbing gold consumption and conserving foreign exchange after the conclusion of the Sino-Indian war of 1962. Desai had hoped gold jewellery would be recycled rather than imported, but he hadn't factored in the Indian passion for 22-karat gold. As it turned out, he achieved nothing beyond driving the gold business underground, and creating a massive black market in precious metals.

Although our showroom had silver jewellery on display, customers who were interested in gold jewellery could make a specific request; only then were the gold items brought out for their inspection. This was the standard practice among jewellers at the time, and indeed, was the only feasible method.

The Gold Control Act of 1968 introduced reforms, relaxing the regulations to a great extent. Licensed retailers were permitted to stock two kilograms of gold per artisan in their employ. Goldsmiths could hold up to a hundred grams on a licence. The ban on jewellery of more than 14-karat gold was lifted. However, private citizens could not own gold bars and coins; these had to be declared and converted into jewellery.

As always, Appan acted swiftly. No sooner did he hear on the radio that the Gold Control Bill had been tabled than he made arrangements for experienced artisans and applied for a licence on the strength of his existing jewellery business.

Securing the licence, which was to be issued by the Central Excise and Customs Department (CECD), proved to be a herculean task. In those days, the CECD had vast powers that allowed it to conduct raids, confiscate goods and even arrest erring individuals. Besides, India was still under licence raj, and government departments were known for red tape.

After several visits to Calicut (now Kozhikode) in pursuit of his licence, Appan learnt that his application had been rejected. He persevered and wrote a petition to the commissioner, CECD. He followed it up with numerous visits to their office, which were often marked by arguments and confrontations. At times, he would return home disappointed and deeply distressed by his tribulations in Calicut. But he never gave up.

Finally, his unceasing efforts paid off, and in September 1971, the CECD granted Alukkas the licence to operate a jewellery business, based on Appan's previous experience. His persistence was rewarded. For me, the lesson from his ordeal was sheer determination in the pursuit of a goal. Never give up, not even when the odds are stacked against you. Only then can you actualize your dreams.

At the time, licenced gold retailers were few, and most of them were in Thrissur. Customers from all over the state came there to purchase ornaments, the reason being that virtually every auspicious occasion—wedding, anniversary, childbirth and festival, such as Thrissur Pooram—involves gifts of gold. Kerala brides famously wear more gold on average than anywhere else in the country.

Jewellery retail functioned differently in the 1970s and 1980s, given that the stock was limited. In sharp contrast to the massive showrooms today, ex-stock delivery was rare. Usually, a customer selected a design from a catalogue or brochure, or explained his requirements, and then placed an order. The customer might say, 'I want to place an order for one chain, two bangles and two rings.' The ornaments would be handmade according to the specifications, involving a delay of days or weeks, depending on the size of the order. The Alukkas store's main competition at the time comprised a handful of jewellery stores, including Chiriankandath, Chettupuzha Paul and Mathew, Thottan and C.A. Ouseph.

Right at the outset, Appan was faced with the all-important question: the naming of the store. He had thought long and hard before dispensing with our long family name, Puthussery-Alukka, and replacing it with Alukkas. Firstly, it was short and would be easy to remember. Secondly, he wanted to effectively hide a fact that few people were aware of: we were not natives of Thrissur, but outsiders. Hiding our provenance would have been impossible had he persisted with our original family name. It was a time when family names carried weight. While this had not mattered much in the textile and umbrella businesses, it was of the utmost essence in the gold sector. To survive in the jewellery business, one's name had to be worth its weight in gold.

In naming the showroom Alukkas, I suspect Appan was inspired by Chakolas. He was often seen staring at the Chakolas board near our radio agency. The Chakolas were one of the few rich families in Thrissur at the time, and were a byword in the city. Alukkas conveyed credibility—very important in a jeweller—and being short and mellifluous, was memorable. Of course, he couldn't have known then that he was laying the foundations of a global brand for decades to come.

Jack of All Trades

The Alukkas scions were initiated into business while still in school. My father stationed his sons in his various enterprises. One of my brothers sat in the stationery shop, another took care of umbrella manufacturing, and a third had been positioned at the radio agency. As for me, I was the family workhorse.

I was outdoors for the most part, running errands or acting as courier. My sisters would say, 'Other brothers full time in shop, Joy full time out.' All five brothers had sharply contrasting personalities and tended to pull in different directions, all the while vying with each other for dominance. My brothers were content to man the shops, but I was happiest outdoors. My distaste for sedentary jobs had little to do with the age difference between me and my older brothers; it was a matter of temperament.

From the very beginning, I was averse to authority and disinclined to taking orders—as I would have had to do in the showroom, given my junior status in the family hierarchy. Under my father's aegis, I had freedom of thought because as long as I performed my duties, he was never judgmental. I was constantly questioning the status quo. To my mind, running a business called for a flexible approach, as there was always room for improvement. My brothers, by contrast, were comfortable with tried-and-tested methods, and did not lend an ear to my ideas. So, I preferred to give them a wide berth, and kept my thoughts to myself.

My early experiences in life may have made me an independent thinker, but most importantly, a problem-solver. Indeed, the person that I am today, every skill that I possess, goes back to my youth. All through those years, I was Appan's shadow, so I had the advantage of being exposed to valuable learnings in a variety of fields. For instance, I learnt a lot about agriculture, because I would accompany Appan when he visited our agricultural land in the Cheroor area of Thrissur. I performed various tasks related to its cultivation assigned to me with diligence, from preparing the field for sowing to post-harvest management.

When I grew older, my responsibilities were extended to organizing family functions. Chief among these were the weddings of my many sisters. Every year, one of them would get married. I would plan and execute the event, attending to the endless details of church arrangements, the choir, the priest and the invitations. I would also organize the panthal (tent), chairs, tables, crockery, cutlery and cooking vessels, borrowing what I could and hiring the rest.

The family began to take it for granted that all outdoor activities like construction, supervising the umbrella unit at night or logistics—picking up and delivering consignments—were part of my domain. I was particularly happy to assist my father in his real estate ventures. There was hardly any competition in the field at that time, with only a couple of players.

Appan had a keen eye for properties with good potential. Purchasing land, developing colonies and building villas and houses on empty plots was a source of gratification for him. He enjoyed both the construction and the business aspects. A self-taught architect, he had an instinctive insight on layout. Working with him, I became well-versed in architectural design.

Most of the land we developed had once been under paddy, a highly water-intensive crop. Building structurally sound homes and solid foundations on wet soil was by no means simple. I learnt on site how to gauge the quality of bricks and strength of steel, the precise proportions of mortar used in different applications, and a hundred other things that can only be imbibed through experience. It was capsule education in civil engineering.

The learning curve was steep but exhilarating, beginning with the purchase and clearing of land, to the stage-by-stage construction of residential units. I also acquired a sound grasp of labour relations, a vital skill in Kerala. All in all, watching thirty or so villas materialize seemingly out of thin air seemed to satisfy my creative urge, and my fascination with the technical aspects of construction. An added thrill was striking deals for the sale of those villas.

But most of all, I enjoyed the freedom to make decisions on my own. If I made a mistake, I could course-correct without worrying about my judgmental seniors. I was accountable only to my father, who was a strict parent and a tough taskmaster, but was always fair.

The Freebie Faux Pas

I had occasion to test Appan's sense of fairness when I worked up the courage to approach him on the delicate subject of pocket money. Given that I went to work immediately after classes, I was always hungry by evening. My brothers, stationed in the shops, doubtless ordered tea when they felt like it, but I didn't have that luxury.

Approaching my father, I said tentatively, 'I need some money.'

'What for?'

'Coffee money, Appan. I get so hungry that it becomes hard to concentrate on the job. If you give me, say, twenty-five paise every day, I will be able to buy something to eat.'

My father nodded. 'Certainly, you must have some money, if it will help you concentrate on your work better.'

From then on, I received twenty-five paise every day, which proved quite adequate. Bus fares were low—the ticket from Thrissur to Ollur, a distance of around nine kilometres, costed just five paise. I could get a cup of tea and two kinds of snacks (fried bananas were my favourite) for ten paise. On the flip side, my newfound wealth inadvertently created a problem in the umbrella unit.

Inspired by my request, Appan decided to motivate his workers by giving them 'coffee money' as well. It was a pioneering move, and worked well for a while. With a Communist regime in place, workers' rights were a hot topic of discussion in all walks of society. Inevitably, a mindset of entitlement trickled in, and our workforce began to regard the incentive as part of their due. They went on strike, demanding a 20 per cent increase in their coffee money.

It was a valuable lesson. I learned that every benefit given to one's employees ought to be a part of their emoluments, so that they value it as something they deserve and have earned.

The gesture was typical of my father, a God-fearing man with a strong philanthropic streak. Not only did he look after his own siblings, but my mother's as well, although she was not the eldest child in her family. His protective umbrella extended to my maternal aunts and uncles, who became very close to us as a result.

Despite having an army of his own offspring to support, he had a strong instinct for serving his fellow man. He could not bear to see anyone go hungry, be it a pauper or a committee chairman. He would often chat with outstation customers, and invariably ask, 'Have you eaten?' If the individual in question shook his head, his secretary, Krishna Nair, would be immediately summoned and told: 'Nair, go and get some food for these people.'

On one occasion, I recall Nair being told to give 'bus money' to a youth. Apparently, the lad had run away from home and Appan had persuaded him to go back.

Both Appan and Amma believed that giving succour to the ailing and needy was a humanitarian duty. So often did they visit the sick that they became well-acquainted with the geography and staff of government hospitals in Thrissur. Despite their busy schedules, they always found time not only to attend church but to get involved in church-related activities.

Open-handed and benevolent on the one hand, my father was a stickler for increasing profits and keeping accounts on the other. As a child, I found it difficult to reconcile what seemed like two opposing aspects of his nature. Later, I realized that there was no dichotomy; his value system decreed that you did your best in the profession that fate had assigned to you, and at the same time, you served your fellow man. Both were god's work.

Each night, at 8 p.m., the Alukkas brothers would be asked to furnish him with the accounts of the day. If the numbers wouldn't add up or if we had incurred losses, a tongue-lashing would follow. The amount did not matter; he was as upset by a loss of ten rupees as by one of thousand rupees. But he was always fair, and was willing to overlook a genuine mistake, provided it was a first offence.

One time, when I was in the fourth standard, my father had given me ten rupees to make a purchase. I had lost the money, and was terrified of telling him, but decided to make a clean breast of it even before he asked me. 'Appan, I have lost the money you had given me. I have searched everywhere, but cannot find it.'

'Money gone, yes?'

'Yes, Appan. I am very sorry.'

'Money worth one sack of mangoes, gone!'

He did not say another word, but the message had hit home. I had lost money that could have bought a whole sack of mangoes for the family. After that salutary lesson, I was very careful with the cash he entrusted to me.

Other than asking for pocket money, I never made a fuss about the various tasks assigned to me. It might suit other members of my family to characterize me as a good-for-nothing gadabout, but the fact is that I believed—and still do—that even the smallest job must be accomplished to the best of your ability.

After Alukkas reopened, it naturally became our focus. My brothers headed straight to the jewellery showroom after classes—Jos and Paul were in charge of it—while I ran errands for my father. None of us ever got back home before 8 p.m., unless it was a Sunday. I was grateful to the Lord for many things, but most of all that Sunday was designated as a rest day.

One of the most important tasks I was assigned on a regular basis was liaising with the goldsmiths (craftsmen) who manufactured our jewellery. As a learning experience, it was very valuable. It involved an intimate knowledge of the metal—for example, how gold of different purities behaved under various temperatures—as well as the economics of jewellery manufacture and retail. A great deal of mental math was called for, as gold prices were variable and calculators were rare.

At the time, jewellery was handmade. For instance, to make a gold bangle, the artisan would first cast a tube, then make small cuts along its length, before bending it into shape. So skilled were they that the joints were barely discernible to the naked eye. Likewise, gold chains were manually crafted.

Pressure on the goldsmith increased during the wedding season, when there was always a backlog of orders, and customers were impatient to take delivery well in advance of the event. My brothers, who were managing the store, would ask for more time. 'Sir, that is very short notice. Our goldsmiths have their hands full. Please give us another week.'

Often, the customer would reply that he could not afford to wait. Jos and Paul had no choice but to comply, for fear that the customer would threaten to go elsewhere. If Appan learnt of it, he would rap out a general command: 'Go to the goldsmith and stand on his head to make sure that the order is ready on time!'

I would shuttle between the goldsmith's place of work and the showroom to ensure that the orders were filled. A Rajdoot motorcycle was my mode of transport; a necessity, considering the large distances I had to cover. I had to keep a very close eye on quality control, because Appan's standards were high. When I set up my own venture many years later, I emulated his customer-centric approach and emphasis on quality.

The Alukkas store acquired a good reputation and flourished, keeping pace with the rapid growth of the jewellery retail sector in Kerala. In 1980, Alukkas shifted to a more upmarket location on the Thrissur Municipal Office Road, on the erstwhile site of Appan's umbrella store. It was a much larger space and generated better sales. To give credit where it is due, the resources for the new store came from chit funds, which was Paul's idea.

My father had founded the Alukkas store. It was he who had identified the opportunity, arranged funding, hired the staff, found the location, decided on the brand name and ideated the strategy. Once it was established on a firm footing, however, he voluntarily withdrew from the day-to-day operations and handed the business over to his sons, serving only as a mentor.

Effectively, this meant that the mantle fell on Jos. He was twenty-six years old by the time Alukkas got its official licence (in 1971), while Paul was eighteen, and Francis sixteen. As the oldest son, possessed of a strong frame and a naturally aggressive personality, Jos was the top dog from day one.

Business Sense and Sensibility

Every morning, without fail, Appan would share business advice with his sons. His business sense defined him. He lived, breathed and obsessed about business, morning, noon and night. His illuminating lectures were peppered with parables, proverbs, anecdotes and insights drawn from experience. One by one, my siblings would sidle away, leaving me as his sole audience. I didn't mind, because I liked listening to him, and remember his observations to this day.

Of the many things I learned from my father, financial discipline was—and remains—of the utmost importance. He repeatedly emphasized that 'finance is the lifeline of any business', so a 'core understanding of finance is mandatory if one wants to become a great businessman'. To that end, a sound grasp of numbers was essential, he said. He could mentally tabulate the income, expenses, assets and liabilities of all of the various businesses he operated. Numbers were his best friends.

He was a great believer in frugality (except in his charitable efforts) and kept his personal expenses to a minimum. He did not allow himself any luxuries. 'Pala thulli peru vellam' (many a little makes a mickle), he would say, exhorting us to keep track of even the most trifling expenditure. And when it came to negotiating prices with his suppliers, he was uncompromising, no matter how small the amount involved. He acted as if he were as accountable as any of his employees, rather than the proprietor of the business.

Later, I learned through experience that this approach not only helps in cutting overheads but also in inculcating an awareness of financial controls and discipline—not just with respect to employees, but for my children as well.

Appan taught me a measured approach to business decisions. 'Aattil kalanjalum alannu kalayanam' (measure is a treasure), he would say. To this day, I have no hesitation in committing a fortune to a new venture, but the return on investment, in terms of my personal well-being or that of my business, is meticulously calculated beforehand. I am not risk-averse by any means, but again, my decisions when confronted with a speculative proposition are based on a careful reckoning of the projected outcomes.

Another of my father's tenets was financing through loans. At a time when the middle-class were deeply conservative borrowers, he was not averse to debt. The umbrella business was highly seasonal—although manufacturing went on all year around, sales were largely limited to the rainy seasons (Kerala has two monsoons: June to August, and October to November). This put a lot of pressure on working capital.

So, Appan would raise funds to accelerate umbrella manufacturing before the rainy season through borrowings. This included 'key loans' from banks and personal loans from various sources. As soon as the season was over, the money accruing from sales was used to settle with his creditors. I remember how restless he was until he had repaid every last loan.

Paying creditors on time, preferably before the due date, was his abiding principle. As a result, he pointed out to me, they did not hesitate to lend to us again. This translated into long-term trust and work associations. In short, he taught me that debt is not a liability if the funds are used wisely for the business.

This learning was to prove invaluable later in life. When I wanted to expand my business but was strapped for capital, I took a series of tactical and strategic steps to attract loans in order to fuel our company's growth. The expansion of my business has always been on the strength of borrowed money.

Conversely, my father was cautious when extending credit to customers, although it was the norm in the umbrella business. Having been faced with several bad debts during his entrepreneurial career, he didn't believe in it. 'Cash is gold. Don't give credit; it is a bad practice,' he would say.

Once, Jos got into trouble for giving credit to a customer he did not know.

'Who is this person to whom you have given credit?' my father asked.

'His name is Moustache Antony,' replied Jos.

'What kind of name is Moustache Antony? Who is this person?'

'His first name is Antony and he has a moustache,' explained my brother, adding, 'we have his signature.' Jos was thoroughly nervous by this time.

'Fetch it,' my father snapped.

The customer's signature turned out to be illegible. 'Can you make out his family name?' asked Appan.

Jos shook his head.

'Then how will you recognize him?'

'By his moustache?'

My father laughed. 'One day, the moustache will be gone. Then, won't the money also be gone?'

Jos had no reply, so he just hung his head.

I took no satisfaction in Jos' discomfiture—after all, any of us could have been in his shoes. I had made my own share of mistakes. But I internalized the lesson Appan had sought to impart to his sons, and have always been cautious when extending credit.

According to Appan, the four pillars of a business are: quality control, rigorous compliance (everything has to be done through legal channels, in strict conformity with regulations), price discovery and excellent customer service.

He never compromised on the quality of products. Every aspect of umbrella manufacturing, for instance, was explained to his workers in minute detail so that it was clear to even the meanest intelligence. I remember his training sessions, during which he would pick up a sample umbrella, open it and explain the quality parameters.

He would point at the canopy. 'Look at the cloth from which it is made. See the mark. This is first-class Century mill cloth, so not even a drop of water will go inside. Now look at the iron frame, with the long ribs and the short ribs. This is a frame made by the Champion company. It will not bend easily. Here is the shaft. It is chromium-plated, so it will not rust,' he would say.

To sum up my father's philosophy in a sentence: he put business before self.

After my academic career came to a premature end, I began to work with my father full-time. As always, I was the itinerant one, ever ready to hop onto my motorcycle in pursuit of some task or the other. I worked hard, but I also played hard, and managed to find time for travel and adventure. One of those exploits remains etched in my memory forever.

3

Cashless in Kashmir, and Other Adventures

The most thrilling adventure of my youth was inspired by a Hindi film. The 1973 box-office hit *Bobby* had a cult following among young adults in Kerala, courtesy its 'star-crossed lovers' theme. For me, the allure of the film owed less to the rapturous love story than the exquisite locales where it had been shot.

The stunning snowscape of Kashmir's Gulmarg, captured in the '*Hum tum ek kamre mein band hon*' song sequence, had caught my imagination. The image stayed with me, and I was determined that I would see the snows for myself one day. Once I had made up my mind, I usually followed through, regardless of how long it might take or how tough the journey might be.

The opportunity cropped up in the winter of 1978 when my friends, all of whom were in college, had finished their exams and were awaiting their results. We were a big group, numbering some twenty-two youngsters from well-reputed families. The 'gang' members, apart from me, included Joy Daniel, Prince Immatty and Chackochan A.R. All, except for me, were graduate students in different colleges in Thrissur. I was the only one who had an occupation, but apart from my inner circle, everyone thought that I, too, was enrolled in college.

We met almost every day, congregating at around 5 p.m. for masala dosas and coffee at the Triveni restaurant near the Paramekkavu temple. I would come straight from work on my Rajdoot. After the light meal, we would adjourn to the Thrissur Pooram round, also known as the Thekkinkadu Maidanam, where we discussed the news of the day over roasted peanuts.

The Thrissur Pooram round played a significant role in our lives, serving not just as a rendezvous point, but as a dipstick of current affairs and public sentiments. It was a place where all manner of people met in the evenings, to exchange gossip and discuss the vital questions of the day.

Apart from the Thrissur Pooram round, our favourite meeting spots were the CIP Lodge and the Soni Lodge. I was not involved in student politics, although several of my friends were. Then, as now, the Congress and the Left were at loggerheads ideologically, but political debates were never acrimonious.

We were all in the first flush of youth, with limited pocket money and strict, conservative parents who had set a curfew of 8 p.m. My compatriots explained their absence from home before that time by citing 'tuitions' and 'group studies'. I had no such excuse, but then, I rarely needed one. As long as I accomplished the tasks I was assigned, my parents did not question my movements. My hours were flexible out of necessity; when my father handed me an assignment, there was no telling how long it would take to execute it.

Like youngsters the world over, we were always short of money. Typically, we pooled our resources to meet restaurant bills. The contributions varied according to the state of a member's pocket, and we always seemed to have enough for our daily sessions of tea and snacks. I, as a member of the workforce, had more money than most.

On that particular evening in 1978, the topic of discussion was a post-exam vacation. Various destinations were discussed, notably Bangalore (now Bengaluru) and Goa, but my mind was made up: I wanted to go to Kashmir.

My friends were hesitant, because it was so far away—farther from Thrissur than Dubai, as the crow flies. Always ripe for adventure, I pointed out that it would be the thrill of a lifetime. None of us had ever seen snow, or been to the north of India. This was the one opportunity we had to explore it together. All we had to do was take a long train ride each way, up and down the length of India. There would be so much to see and learn, so many unique experiences to recount.

In short, I convinced them, or at least two of them, namely Jerry Chandy and Uthuppu Attokran. I don't know what my friends told their families, but I informed mine that I was joining my college friends on a short trip that had been organized by the institution itself, and did not mention our destination.

The three of us bought tickets for the Himsagar Express, which ran from Kanyakumari to Jammu, at a cost of seventy-three rupees per head. I was left with the princely sum of Rs 4,500, while the others had a couple of thousand between them, so we were quite confident that we had enough money to cover the entire trip. As always, we were going to pool our resources.

We packed light—one small bag each, crammed with newly purchased trousers and shirts—and the three of us boarded the Himsagar Express in a spirit of exhilaration. I was wearing trousers, rather than a dhoti, for the first time in my life.

The entire group thronged the Thrissur railway station. We stood by the door of our coach, watching them disappear. The train jerked forward and rolled out of the station. Our adventure had begun.

Fire and Snow

A few hours later, we became aware of the first lapse in our planning. We had not carried food or water. In those days, there were no vendors selling mineral water, cold drinks or packaged snacks. Luckily for us, our co-passengers proved to be very friendly and made sure that we were watered and fed all through the shared journey.

As the train headed northwards, one of the passengers, a native of Thrissur, advised us to stop over at Agra. 'It is on the way,' he said. 'You should break journey for at least a day to visit the Taj Mahal.' We had not known that the train stopped at Agra. Now that we did, it seemed like a golden opportunity to see one of the most famous monuments in the world.

We decided to take our co-passenger's advice. At the time, it was possible to break journey and then board the same train a few days later, without incurring additional charges. So, when the train pulled into the Agra Cantonment station, we quickly scrambled out on to the platform.

We emerged from the station onto a busy thoroughfare. Immediately, rickshaw-wallahs converged on us, clamouring for our custom. We shook our heads, but they continued to hound us, so we boarded the first bus that passed by. A few stops later, we got off and looked around for a tonga (horse-drawn buggy) that could take us to the Taj Mahal.

Jerry spotted a tonga-wallah and approached him, saying, 'We want to go to the Taj Mahal. How much will you charge?'

'Nabbe (ninety) paise,' the man replied in Hindi.

Unfamiliar with Hindi numerals, we made a counter offer in English: 'We will give one rupee.'

'Nabbe paise,' he insisted. His understanding of English was obviously as poor as ours of Hindi.

Unaware that we were offering more than his asking price, we stuck to our guns. After wrangling for several minutes, he yielded and gestured that we should hop into the tonga.

'Hee-ya,' he shouted at the horse, and the tonga rolled ahead, winding its way through busy streets. We enjoyed the ride, arriving all too soon at our destination. The tonga turned a corner, and there it was, the Taj Mahal, in all its pearly white glory. Our co-passenger had been right; it was definitely worth a visit. We descended from the tonga, wide-eyed and wonder-struck, and walked around the marble monument and the surrounding gardens for hours.

We resumed our journey, but en route from Delhi to Jammu, the train ran into a 'rail roko' (stop the train) protest by supporters of former prime minister Indira Gandhi, who had been arrested on the orders of the then home minister,

Chaudhary Charan Singh. The train halted for six hours, so we reached Jammu late that night. We found a small hotel, and fell asleep immediately. After a hearty breakfast the following morning, we caught a bus to Srinagar. The seven-hour bus ride gave us ample time to enjoy the mountainous vista.

The moment we disembarked at Srinagar, a glacial chill enveloped us. Dusk was falling, and the sun was a reedy thread of vermillion in the sky. Beautiful though the sunset was, it seemed to enhance the cold. So far, ensconced for the most part in a train or a bus, we had not really felt the icy bite of winter.

It was only then that we realized our folly in not having brought any woollens. Had we discussed our plans with our elders, they might have ensured that we were better prepared for the intense cold of a north Indian winter. I had packed a canvas coat, naively imagining that it would protect me from the chill. I didn't know then that it would be less useful than a broom in a dust storm.

As we shivered at the bus stand, a man approached us, offering a houseboat for hire. Before we could answer, another appeared with the same offer. Soon, we were surrounded by agents, each one promising a good deal on a houseboat.

As scions of successful business families, we assessed the lowest rate before giving the nod to one of the agents. He took us to the Dal Lake, frozen and grey in the dusk. Chilled to the bone, we huddled around a fire on the embankment and shared a hookah with the local denizens. Meanwhile, our agent went off to strike a deal with the owner of the houseboat.

The interior of the houseboat was no warmer than the lake shore. It was furnished with wooden chairs and beds.

The owner had provided wood for a fire, but it was not enough to see us through the night. Our thin apparel offered no protection whatsoever, and by this time, it was too late to go shopping for warm clothes.

'I can't bear this cold,' said Jerry. 'I feel as if I am going to freeze to death.'

'You are right,' agreed Uthuppu. 'We must do something to get warm.'

We must have been suffering from brain freeze, because we came up with an idea that was as outrageously stupid as it was practical. We needed to keep the fire burning. The fire needed wood. Chairs are made of wood. So, we fed them into the fire. A fierce blaze went up, and we revelled in the heat.

The following morning, the owner paid us a visit and discovered that his chairs had been reduced to charred fragments. He was understandably upset and demanded compensation. We had no choice but to comply. After we had settled accounts with him, very little of our holiday money remained.

Our situation was now truly pathetic: we were at the mercy of the elements, in inadequate clothing and with very little money. We did not have the funds to buy ourselves warm clothing. Somehow, we made our way to Gulmarg. As the Himalayan vistas unfolded before us, it all seemed to have been worth it. The views were stunning, like a dream sequence from a Bollywood film. And yes, we did manage to see the house where '*Hum tum ek kamre mein*' had been shot.

Our mission accomplished, we headed back to Jammu. What little money we had left was spent on bus tickets to New Delhi. Looking back, I marvel at the naivety of youth.

It never once occurred to us to call up our parents in Kerala and ask them to send us money. We went to the New Delhi railway station, and boarded the train to Thrissur. Coming from reputed families, we disliked the idea of ticketless travel, but there was no choice. Fortunately, we found soldiers from Kerala who were heading home on the same train, and they gave us some food.

It was a long, hard journey with barely any sustenance. By the time we reached Thrissur—three weeks after we had left home—I was exhausted and weak. Also, having told my parents that it would be a 'short trip', I was very anxious about the reception I would receive at home. As it turned out, my absence had not been noticed. In fact, my mother's opening words when she saw me that morning were: 'Aren't you going to the showroom?'

Did I regret having gone on that journey? Not at all. It had been a revelation for me; there was so much to see, experience and understand outside of Thrissur. I had always been restless, and now, an urge to travel and see the world was born. Appan had always said that a formal education does not equip one to navigate the real world, because there is no substitute for experience.

He was right; my adventure had taught me the importance of practical survival skills, cultural competence and emotional resilience. No matter how hopeless your circumstances seem to be, and how helpless you feel, the best way forward is to take action. To shake off the feeling of despair and get up and do something, instead of waiting for a solution or a grand stroke of luck.

I also had the satisfaction of having inspired my friends to take the voyage of discovery. They came back with a feeling of confidence, having accomplished what they had thought was impossible. This ability to inspire people to push themselves beyond their limits would stand me in good stead throughout my life.

Our odyssey had been a leap into the unknown, without resources, support systems or prior knowledge of the terrain. We had put ourselves through a tough trial, and had emerged from it with a sense of achievement. As Barack Obama was to say decades later, 'Yes, we can!'

Searching for Stars

Our Kashmir adventure was by no means our first foray outside Kerala. Prior to that, we had ventured into the neighbouring state of Tamil Nadu in search of what was then a holy grail for us: face-time with film stars.

For all our enchantment with the Bollywood romantic genre epitomized by *Bobby,* none of us had a girlfriend. The scope for romance was limited, given that we all came from conservative Christian families. Social barriers apart, it would have been impossible to arrange secret trysts in a town where everybody knew everybody. As my friend Babu said, we were 'Thrissurian in our habits', by which he meant that we were all from upper-middle-class families, steeped in religion and conservative in our attitudes. One worked hard, did one's duty and waited for the family elders to find an approved bride.

We perforce sublimated our romantic yearnings into fantasies woven around film stars. Chief among our heartthrobs were the dewy-eyed Sharada, star of the 1972 hit film *Swayamvaram,* and Sheela, the female lead in *Chemmeen,* another popular and much-awarded film. We also idolized actor Madhavan Nair aka Madhu, who had starred in both films as the leading man. We loved the cinema, and we loved Madhu, Sharada and Sheela. The beauteous Sharada was not from Kerala—she was born Saraswathi Devi in Tenali, Andhra Pradesh—but she had found fame and acclaim in the Malayalam film industry. We counted ourselves as die-hard fans of all three stars. Drunk on tea and teenage bravado, we resolved to meet them. We were convinced that we would somehow manage to get photographed with them and get their autographs.

As the popular Malayalam film magazine *Nana* noted, most Malayalam films were shot in Kodambakkam city near Madras (now Chennai). So central was Kodambakkam to the film industry that those who aspired to become part of it would relocate there permanently. We figured that with all the actors roaming around the city, it would be easy to see them all in one go.

We travelled to Madras by train, in a first-class coupe on the Madras Mail. En route, we met the famous Malayalam playback singer, Jayachandran. All night long, we stayed up to listen to his songs and chat with him. Our journey was off to a promising start! The next morning, we reached Madras Central railway station and hired a cycle-rickshaw to roam around the city. The highlight of the tour was the famous Marina Beach.

On the following day, we travelled to Kodambakkam, just about ten kilometres away from Madras. We tried our luck at various studios, but were not allowed inside. Unfortunately, none of us had any contacts in the film industry who could secure us entry. We returned to Thrissur the next day, with no regrets.

Madhu, Sharada and Sheela, it seemed, were destined to remain an elusive dream. Our love for cinema—and our infatuation—continued regardless. As often as our funds allowed, we would gather outside the Casino hotel and head to the theatre, to sigh over the leading actors of the day.

The abortive attempt to meet our favourite film stars was our first excursion to Tamil Nadu. Our next trip was to Coimbatore, where we went to watch the team from Kerala participating in the Santosh Trophy, the national football championship, held under the aegis of the All India Football Federation. One of the gang members, Isaac, persuaded us to go, because Kerala's football team featured several players from Thrissur, including M.M. Jose, who was a local celebrity. We embarked on three motorcycles—my Rajdoot, a Jawa and an Enfield Bullet—on what was to prove an exhilarating trip. The match was a cliff-hanger, well worth the effort of travelling, and we shouted ourselves hoarse. At Coimbatore, we also watched the first show of the Hindi film *Qurbani*, which had just been released.

Another of our favourite topics of discussion, apart from film divas and football, was travel. The furthest any of us had ever gone was my (in)famous trip to Jammu and Kashmir, but we dreamed of touring America, Europe and the Gulf countries. The latter seemed most accessible.

The Gulf Gold Rush

The Gulf oil boom of the 1970s triggered a mass migration of workers from Kerala to West Asia, bringing wealth to our shores. A sizeable chunk of these remittances was invested in gold, and Alukkas was to take advantage of the 'gold rush' by opening a second jewellery showroom in Calicut, approximately nineteen years after the first.

Another outcome of the Kerala–Gulf boom was a flood of foreign goods. Returning home on holidays, the 'Gulf Man' brought with him electronic gadgets, watches, perfumes, clothes and accessories, jewellery and all manner of bric-a-brac. These items were available for sale and denizens of Thrissur were happy to buy them. For me, the fascination of foreign-made goods lay in what they represented: the siren call of countries overseas, where I could perhaps someday strike out on my own. The idea was subliminal, just below the surface of my consciousness, but it was there.

My friends and I would make a monthly trip to the 'Kochu Dubai' (mini Dubai) of Chavakkad beach in search of foreign goods for ourselves or our families. We would set off in a convoy of three cars and stop at a toddy shop en route to pick up two bottles of country liquor. We would then head to a secluded beach and make ourselves comfortable on the sand. We had a portable Sony cassette player that ran on six batteries, and we would switch it on at full volume to belt out the popular tracks of the day, mostly disco beats like 'Funkytown' by Lipps Inc. The bottles of toddy would pass from hand to hand as we danced with abandon against the salty sea spray.

If the sun proved too overpowering, we would dive into the blue-grey waters of the Arabian Sea, swimming against the foam-capped waves until we had worked off all the alcohol in our systems. Sometimes, when the sea was calm, we would just float idly on our backs, eyes closed, listening to the whisper of the waves.

Ours was a charmed generation, growing up as we did in the seventies and eighties. Dancing in dhotis and kurtas on beaches in all-male gatherings was not considered odd at the time. As long as these get-togethers were innocent and remained within the ambit of social mores, our families raised no objection. To our credit, we stayed within the bounds of their expectations.

Most of us had a sense of our future, which lay in our respective family businesses. Some of my friends would go into banking, because their families had been in finance for generations. Others, like me, would be involved in other sectors, be it real estate, manufacturing or retail—whatever the family patriarch decided.

'Too Many of Us'

Not all my friends met with my father's approval. He had taken to spending a large part of his Sundays on a reclining chair in the living room, poring over newspapers. The chair was his alone and nobody else ever dared to sit on it. From this vantage point, he would survey my friends when they came over. After a long and critical scrutiny, those he did not like would be sent away forthwith. Appan would say coldly, 'Why have you come? Joy is very busy. Go, go! You can meet him some other time.'

Those who passed muster would be engaged in small talk. 'Ah! You're studying in college? Good, good! Education is very important these days. What does your father do? Oh! You are so-and-so's son. I know him very well. Good man! You want to meet Joy? He's inside. Go in, go in. I'm sure he will be very happy to see you.'

Despite my father's penchant for diversifying his business, the M.O. Road showroom remained the jewel in the Alukkas crown. But it soon became obvious that the business was not large enough to accommodate all five Alukkas brothers. Francis saw a way out. One day, as the family was eating dinner, he said, 'I think it's time for us to open up another jewellery store.'

This was a startling suggestion, as jewellery showrooms were standalone in those days. The idea of starting operations in a different city was a novel one.

My father asked why. Francis replied, 'There are already too many of us in the M.O. Road store. It's not big enough for all of us.'

When Appan admitted his sons as partners in the family business in 1980, Jos was thirty-five, while Paul was twenty-seven and Francis was twenty-five. They were the decision-makers. Although I was only a year younger than Francis, at twenty-four, my opinion did not count for much. Nor did Anto's, who was twenty-one. Later, I learnt that my father had been deeply hurt when he sent an aide to get some cash from the Thrissur showroom, only to be told that Jos had turned him away.

Personally, I didn't agree with Appan's decision to give shares in the business to his sons, particularly because after he did so, Jos tended to overlook his opinions more often than not.

Many years later, when I had my own business, I decided that my assets would be passed on to my children only after I had called it a day. In any case, I do not believe that they should inherit all of the wealth I have built up. How much money does a person need after all? I have already put plans in motion to follow my father's footsteps through philanthropic endeavours. A substantive share of my wealth will be devoted to this cause.

Appan usually kept his distance from the jewellery business, except to offer advice. He turned to Francis and said, 'You may be right, there are too many of you in Thrissur. But how do we know that the new store will succeed?'

Francis was firm. 'I think if we start a store in Calicut, it will do very well. A lot of Gulf money is coming in there, and most of it is going into gold,' he said. He went on to explain that he was prepared to shift to Calicut; a family business needed the family touch. My father was clearly impressed with Francis's reasoning. 'You are correct. Calicut is a growing market for gold jewellery. Not only because of Gulf money, but because farmers have started making money from exports,' he said. The global price of Malabar garbled pepper, a major cash crop of the region, was going north (over the next five years, the price was to triple), putting disposable income in the hands of the landowners.

Appan and Jos both agreed to the new store, on the understanding that Francis would move to Calicut and manage it. My brother was instructed to go there at once and find a suitable site for the proposed jewellery showroom.

Then, once the location had been finalized, Jos surprised us all by saying, 'Take Joy with you. He will be your assistant.' It was the first time I had been given such importance in the jewellery business. I looked at Francis, who seemed quite happy with the idea. The two of us had become quite close, because Francis was very accommodative. He listened to my opinions and allowed me to have a flexible schedule and to make my own choices, whether professional or personal.

I was given to understand that from then on, I would have to divide my time between the two towns. For the next two years, I did just that.

Paul's contribution was the idea of funding the new store through chits (a sort of peer-to-peer banking and lending, very popular in Kerala). On 21 September 1983, Alukkas opened on M.M. Ali Road, Calicut. I had decided to launch it with a party for my friends, near Peechi Dam. It was a final splash, a toast to the carefree days of our youth.

We were all young men now, poised to step into the next phase of our lives. As we sought to find our feet in the adult world as productive members of society, all of us were conscious that we were on the verge of entering uncharted waters: matrimony. The prospect was simultaneously daunting and enticing. For me, it was more of the latter. In fact, there was nothing I desired more than to be married.

4

Love, Death and Golden Dreams

She wore a gold-bordered white silk sari that brought out the dusky gold of her complexion, and through the sheer veil pinned to her hair with flowers, I saw that she had big brown eyes and full lips, quivering with nerves. My first glimpse of the girl I was to marry was at our wedding in St. Joseph's Church. At once, I was in love.

She took the last few steps down the aisle towards me, her head bowed. I couldn't take my eyes off her. As she stood beside me, I kept glancing at her surreptitiously.

We marked the commencement of the wedding ceremony by lighting a lamp together. Then the priest took over, reading verses from the Bible in Malayalam, and taking us through our wedding vows. When he asked whether we agreed to take each other as man and wife, I didn't hesitate even for a moment.

'I do,' I said, my voice loud and firm.

'I do,' said Jolly, in a softer tone.

The ceremony concluded with the 'minnukettu' ritual. I had to tie the 'minnu'—seven threads from the 'manthrakodi' (marriage sari) presented by the groom to the bride—around her neck, a ritual I performed with my hands shaking. The threads would later be replaced by a gold chain. We then signed our names in the marriage register in the church vestry. We were now officially man and wife.

The wedding ceremony was short, but the road to it had been a long one. The average age of marriage for boys in the Alukkas family was twenty-two, and even before I reached my twenties, I had dreamed of tying the knot with an incandescent girl in fairy-tale fashion, followed by my very own 'happily-ever-after'. All my adolescent yearnings were focused on my unseen, unnamed beloved, and I looked forward to a blissful union. Month after month, I ticked off days on the calendar, anticipating that happy denouement.

Unfortunately for me, my older brother Francis refused to get married, which meant that the rest of us would have to wait our turn. He seemed oblivious of the fact that by postponing his nuptials, he was creating a bottleneck for his younger siblings. Each year, he would fob my parents off with a curt 'next year'. Every proposal they presented to him was rejected in a firm 'no arguments please' tone. One day, I took him to task.

'Francis, why do you refuse to get married? Why don't you listen to our parents and let them find you a nice girl?' I asked.

Francis was surprised that I, a junior member of the family, had broached the subject with him.

'What difference does it make to you?'

'Look, Francis. All your younger brothers are in the queue. We cannot get married until you do. We are all awaiting our turn.'

'Why are you in such a hurry to get married?'

It was a good question. Why was I so keen to get married? Was it because I was a romantic at heart, or the fact that being a middle child, subjected to constant criticism by my siblings, I wanted someone who would stand by me? All I knew was that ever since my teenage years, I had been desperate for a life partner, whose unquestioning love and loyalty I could count on.

I didn't have an answer, so I shrugged and turned away, resolving to nag him until I wore him down. My family had not yet realized it, but I could be quite obstinate! From that day on, I launched a campaign for Francis' marriage.

Francis kept rejecting proposal after proposal, and my frustration mounted. Then, on one halcyon day, to everyone's surprise, he said 'yes'. Perhaps, he finally felt ready for marriage. No matter, I was overjoyed. Three months later, on a sultry Sunday, Francis exchanged vows with his bride. I had moved one step closer to my goal. Soon, it would be my turn, I told myself.

Over the next few months, I learned that bachelors from families like mine were not quite as eligible as I had imagined. True, our businesses were thriving and we had sizeable real estate assets, not to mention one of the most popular jewellery showrooms in Thrissur, which had gained considerable momentum vis-à-vis its competitors, but our lack of formal education was a serious handicap. Education was seen not only as opening doors to successful careers, but as a marker of social status, and had thus become desirable for both genders.

In this context, my brothers and I were at a disadvantage. Only Paul and Anto had been able to attend college, but neither managed to get a degree as their academic careers were cut short. From the perspective of parents of potential brides, the rest of us failed to check an important box. A middle-level businessman could not be trusted to provide a stable income. After all, businesses could fail, but a salary cheque would not. Given a choice between an executive working in a major corporate house and an entrepreneur, they would choose the former.

Marriage brokers ruled the roost in those days. Fixing marriages involved endless rounds of meetings, discussions, home visits and scrutiny. When my turn finally came, I took it for granted that I had no say in the matter, and had no expectation of being asked for my opinion. We had been brought up in a culture where filial duty meant absolute obedience, and this extended to our marriages.

The year 1984 was a significant one. My parents informed me that my bridegroom-in-waiting status was to come to an end. I had only the vaguest idea how this happy state of affairs had come about. The marriage broker had found a girl, and my parents had approved of her. The broker had fixed a date and time for the families to meet, and it had gone well. My sister told me that the girl's name was Jolly. Apparently, the very fact that both our names had their roots in happiness had contributed to the positive outcome.

I was told that Jolly had a bachelor's degree in history, that our fathers had known each other through business, and that she lived in Koratty, a small industrial town in Thrissur district. And that was all I knew about my bride-to-be.

All that remained was to get a formal assent from the bride's family. Much to our surprise (because parents of prospective brides usually took time to decide), Jolly's relatives visited our house within a few days of the initial meeting for the 'orappeeru' (assent to the match). Both our families were prominent and well off, so the question of dowry did not arise. In any event, my father had always been against the system, which was rampant in all the communities in Kerala. My brothers and I naturally supported this view. For us, it was a matter of self-respect; we could support our wives without the aid of our in-laws.

The wedding date and venue were decided, and the invitations printed. I gleaned my next piece of information about Jolly from our wedding card. It was in an attractive shade of beige, with an ecru border and an intricately designed cameo in maroon bearing the legend: 'Joy weds Jolly'. I opened the card and read, 'Our son Joy weds Jolly (daughter of late Sri Rappai, Therukattil Pudukadan House, Koratty)'. Immediately, I felt a wave of compassion for my bride-to-be, who had lost her father. Given the love and awed respect in which I held my own father, I could think of no worse fate. I began to wonder what she was like, this young woman who had suffered such an awful loss. I was impatient to get to know her.

The sacrament ceremony was to take place on Sunday, 16 September, at 12.05 p.m. at St. Joseph's Church, Kuriachira. The church was a stone's throw away from our home, and we had been attending daily mass there ever since I could remember. All the Alukkas weddings were solemnized at this beautiful church, which dated back to 1931.

Even though I was regarded as somewhat of a rebel by the family, it never occurred to me to engineer a clandestine meeting or speak to Jolly over the phone. I was content to wait for our wedding day, albeit with mounting eagerness. My siblings, realizing how impatient I was to get married, subjected me to relentless teasing. 'A watched pot never boils!' they would say with laughter. I maintained a dignified silence, too wrapped up in my forthcoming nuptials to take offence.

The blessed day finally arrived, and we became man and wife. After the ceremony, the women in the family immediately took Jolly away to dress her in the 'manthrakodi'. I resigned myself to a long wait, because I knew from experience—there was a wedding almost every year in our family—that the bride's change of attire took a long time. I found my friends, and they entertained me until Jolly returned, resplendent in her new sari.

The wedding party then shifted to the Chaliserry Hall at East Fort, and celebrations began in earnest. As was the tradition, Jolly and I departed from the venue in a car, to the accompaniment of cheers, good wishes and flashing cameras. We still had not exchanged a single word; it was only later that evening, when we were alone, that we began to get to know each other.

Even as Jolly and I were settling into our marriage, Francis moved to Calicut. Jos and Paul had shifted out with their families to homes of their own much earlier, so Jolly became the only daughter-in-law residing in the house. In those days, social convention dictated that the ideal wife was obedient and looked to her husband for guidance, while being respectful and helpful to her in-laws.

Like all new brides, Jolly went through a short period of adjustment. I had been correct in surmising that she was deeply religious, but Amma's habit of rising at the crack of dawn to attend mass at church astonished and annoyed her. One morning, soon after our wedding, our driver did not show up for work. Amma was in a tizzy, because there was no one to drive her to church. She shouted out to me.

'Joy, are you sleeping? Wake up! Mohan has not arrived. Come out at once. I have to attend the six o'clock mass.'

Jolly and I woke up and peered at our clock. 'It's 5.30 a.m.! It's raining heavily. Amma should go back to sleep and attend prayers later,' Jolly said.

I knew my mother would not stop calling to me until I emerged from our room, so I quickly put on my clothes. 'This is her life. She would be lost without church,' I told Jolly gently. 'You go back to sleep. I will drive her there.'

'But it seems to be a bad thunderstorm. Why is Amma going out in all this thunder and lightning? Why doesn't she stay in for just one day?' Jolly protested. 'She will come back from church, pick up the broomstick and start her chores. I wish she would relax sometimes.'

The thought of Amma relaxing was laughable. I waved goodbye to Jolly and drove my impatient mother to church.

After a while, Jolly won over my parents with her diligence. She did not know how to cook at the time, but she helped Amma in the kitchen. She got into the habit of waking up early, while I was still in bed, to lend a hand in the washing, scraping and cutting of vegetables. After breakfast, she would don a white sari and accompany my mother to church. They would return from attending mass to tackle the chores of the day, which included preparing lunch boxes that would be sent to the office.

Post-marriage, my routine remained much the same. Work kept me away from home until about eight in the evening. I still met my group of friends, although not as often as I used to as a bachelor. I stopped going to the cinema, because I simply did not have the time. The long hours I spent out of the house allowed me to indulge my nicotine habit; I was smoking about ten cigarettes a day, but let Jolly believe that my intake was limited to two.

A month after our wedding, on 31 October 1984, I saw my father break down and cry for the first time in my life.

Tears, Tragedy and a Touch of Bliss

Appan half-ran into the showroom with tears streaming down his cheeks, his breath coming in short gasps. 'Indira Gandhi is dead. Indira Gandhi is dead!' he said tremulously.

My brothers and I stared at him in shock, our minds numbed by the news that the prime minister of India was no more. Someone in the showroom switched on the radio; I didn't see who it was because my attention was focused on Appan. All India Radio stated baldly that Indira Gandhi had breathed her last at the All India Institute of Medical Sciences in New Delhi.

The news was so awful, so unbelievable, that it felt surreal. I couldn't wrap my head around the fact that Mrs Gandhi had been killed by the very people assigned to protect her. We were aghast, bewildered and fearful at the same time. The entire nation will be in turmoil, I thought.

Our immediate concern was to somehow calm Appan down. 'Why don't we take him to watch a film? He needs a distraction,' a showroom staffer suggested. We dispatched a staffer to procure the tickets. He returned with the news that all of the theatres had closed for the day. In effect, not a single movie was playing in the entire town.

If anything, Appan's emotional response to the untimely death of Mrs Gandhi had deepened my bond with him. I had realized, as all children do, that Appan was not invulnerable. The stern patriarch whose approval I had craved all my life had needed me at that moment. His brief display of emotion, the tiny chink in his armour, made me love him all the more.

A couple of months later, it was time for Jolly and me to take our long-overdue honeymoon. We went to Ponmudi, the hill station in the Western Ghats that was known as the 'Kashmir of Kerala', and was a popular honeymoon destination.

We returned to Thrissur refreshed; I to my work and Jolly to her chores. Occasionally, we would escape the house to watch a movie. Nothing disturbed the even temper of our days until one fine day, Jolly gave me a vital bit of news: she was pregnant. We were both delighted, as were my parents. Tradition decreed that the expectant mother go back to her maternal home to await the birth of the child, so Jolly returned to Koratty in the seventh month of her pregnancy. Her mother Mary, brothers George and Pauly and sister Agnes came to fetch her.

Our home was less than forty kilometres from Koratty, so I was able to visit my wife frequently. As the date of delivery drew closer, my excitement mounted, and so did Jolly's anxiety. The women of the family naturally spent a lot of time speculating on the child's gender. Most of them were positive it would be a boy. It didn't matter either way to us, the prospective parents. But Amma, in her innocence, expressed the traditional view that a male child would ensure the continuation of the family lineage, thereby annoying my mother-in-law and my sisters!

Jolly was expected to deliver in mid-October, around the time of the Koratty Muthy Feast dedicated to Mother Mary. This is an annual event celebrated at Koratty's famous St. Mary's Church. That particular year, it was held on 13 October. The festival is one of considerable significance, and people come from far and wide to attend, so Jolly's house was full of visitors. I was there too, and my arrival, she said, doubled her 'Joy'. I was equally happy to see her, after a long gap.

On the evening of 13 October, we made several rounds of the church and its environs, meeting and greeting friends and relatives, and enjoying the display of lights and fireworks while partaking of sweets and ice creams.

All of a sudden, Jolly felt a stab of pain, and surmised that her labour had begun. I helped her into our car and drove to the hospital. En route, we arrived at a T-junction, where I had to take a significant decision. If I turned right, we would arrive at Chalakudy town, where Jolly's obstetrician was located. A left turn would take us to Koratty hospital.

I realized that it wasn't my decision; it was Jolly's. I turned to her and asked which way we should go. My question gave her the option to consider her own comfort levels vis-à-vis the attending medical staff. 'I don't want to go to Chalakudy; the doctor there is very strict and serious. Take me to Koratty hospital,' she decided.

In any case, I thought, Koratty made more sense, given the urgency of the situation, as it was closer than Chalakudy. We reached the hospital and Jolly was admitted. Members of both our families streamed in. Several hours later, at 3.20 p.m. on 14 October 1985, the doctors emerged and announced: 'It's a boy.'

I took my son into my arms for the first time; it was the most magical moment of my life. We hadn't decided on a name for our child in advance. It was Jolly who chose it. He was christened John Paul, in honour of Pope John Paul II. Incidentally, the Pope visited Thrissur the very next year, in 1986.

A Golden Opportunity

When Jolly came back to Thrissur with our firstborn, we shifted to Calicut for a year. I divided my time between work and home, well aware that my responsibilities on both fronts had increased. I felt the need to spread my wings, to strike out on my own and build something far greater.

At this time, NRIs based in the UAE would come to our showrooms in search of jewellery. I gathered that the UAE was fast becoming a gold hub. Often, the customers would share their experiences in the Gulf. I learnt that the Indian diaspora, particularly from Kerala, had become very large. However, the UAE lacked jewellery stores that catered to Indian tastes in terms of design. It was obvious to me that the jewellery industry there was in a nascent stage.

My restlessness intensified. I needed a new challenge, a new adventure. The urge to travel, which had simmered just below the surface of my consciousness ever since my teens, would no longer be denied. Three of my close friends had been talking to me about settling abroad. Their ambitions spurred my own.

Our showroom in Calicut was doing well, thanks to the newfound prosperity of NRIs and spice exporters. Customers came in sizeable groups and sales continued non-stop through the day. It was a medium-sized store, covering about a thousand square feet, with the result that during the marriage season, we were always overcrowded. Only some fifteen to twenty customers could be accommodated at one time, so we introduced a token system, whereby only the bride/bridegroom and one relative could enter the store together. This ensured maximum sales within our limited space. Within a couple of years, we had outperformed our principal competitor, Alapatt Fashion Jewellery.

Our Thrissur store was also doing well, reflecting the growing appetite for jewellery. Customers came from all over the state, and purchasing jewellery became something of an expedition. They would book themselves into a hotel near the showrooms and arrive a day in advance, so that they would be able to gain entry to the store first thing in the morning without having to queue up.

The success of Alukkas in Calicut and Thrissur inspired several other business groups to venture into the jewellery industry. In fact, all the other prominent national jewellery retail chains from Kerala entered the market at around this time. The most prominent among them is the Malabar group. Its founding partner, M.P. Ahammed, acknowledged that the 'growth of Alukkas in Calicut was our actual inspiration to get into this space'.

The house of Alukkas was now stashed with cash, and there was a compelling reason to expand the business and open new showrooms. Nor was there any need to finance new ventures through loans or chit funds. The downside was that income tax rates were phenomenally high, in excess of 50 per cent. This was a major deterrent to expansion.

One of the family's financial advisers strongly urged us to explore the idea of setting up a jewellery business in the Gulf. He pointed out that, with two successful stores, Alukkas now needed to expand and build the brand. As the environment in India was not conducive to new ventures, we should look at Dubai.

The best way forward, he believed, was to take the business transnational. The United Arab Emirates (founded in 1971 in place of the Trucial Sheikhdoms), with their ever-increasing Indian diaspora, presented an attractive investment option. A golden opportunity was beckoning, and Alukkas ought to take advantage of it.

All the brothers agreed that we ought to consider the Gulf as an investment option. But who would go and explore opportunities there? I volunteered immediately. My brothers reacted with scepticism, saying, 'You don't know the business and you don't know the local language. How will you manage?'

The question remained, if not me, who would go? Anto was too young, and the others were occupied with the Thrissur and Calicut showrooms. The fact was that none of them wanted to go, because they lacked my sense of adventure. Unlike me, they were happy in their comfort zone, and had no desire to explore markets overseas. A couple of them might have resented the idea of my going, because they were convinced I did not understand the business, but would certainly not make the trip themselves. I was the only one willing to travel, and they knew it.

Finally, they said, 'Go, then; see for yourself if there is scope for any new business.' Delighted at having gotten the green light, I discussed it with Jolly, and to my surprise, she was thrilled. 'I have always wanted to go to Dubai,' she exclaimed, her eyes shining. 'Several of my classmates are already there.'

I warned her that it would be a difficult life, with no household help, particularly as I would be busy round the clock, scouting for niches in the market and setting up a business. She dismissed my concerns with confidence, saying that she would manage very well. Of course, there was no question of her accompanying me on my first visit. I would send for her when I was settled.

I looked forward to my departure with surging excitement. A whole new world was about to open up for me. I had built an image of Dubai in my head, based entirely on hearsay, and it resembled an El Dorado. Dreams, unfortunately, have a tendency to turn to dust. So it proved for me.

5

Baptism by Fire

The forty-five days I spent in Ras Al-Khaimah, UAE, in the summer of 1986 constituted one of the most difficult phases of my life—a baptism by fire, no less.

I took a flight from Bombay to RAK airport, full of hope and excitement, anticipating my first sight of the Gulf. The moment I landed, my vision of a modern city with soaring towers, gleaming cars and streets paved with opportunity dissolved into the shifting sands. Ras Al-Khaimah turned out to be a small town, with more hutments than buildings, the antithesis of all that I had imagined a desert sheikhdom would be.

I disembarked, clutching a small bag containing two changes of clothes. I had in my pocket a few dirhams, and a scrap of paper with the phone number and address of my only contact in the UAE. There was no one to receive me, so

I dialled the number from a pay phone. It rang and rang, but nobody picked up. What now?

I began walking, in what I hoped was the direction of the city. The heat was scorching, the air so dry that sweat barely had time to form before it evaporated. The sparse traffic I encountered on the way seemed to consist entirely of trucks laden with dates. A taxi trundled up and I hailed it with relief. It was a rattletrap, but it got me to my destination, which turned out to be a small store called N.C. Jewellery, named after its proprietors, Narayanan and Chandran. One of them happened to be the son of a goldsmith who was working with Alukkas in Thrissur.

As soon as the family signed off on my proposed trip to the UAE, the entire Alukkas staff heard about it. The goldsmith approached Jos Chettan, and revealed that his son might be able to help me obtain a visa. I accepted his offer with alacrity, as there were no travel agents at the time, and I was clueless about the procedures involved. Nor did I have any friends or relatives in the UAE to advise me.

For reasons best known to him, the lad in question applied for a 'home driver visa' on my behalf. I think he thought that I was in the UAE for the sole purpose of buying a car, which was not uncommon at the time. Foreign luxury vehicles were unavailable in India, so those desirous of purchasing a pre-owned but nearly new high-end car would hop across to the UAE, find a desirable vehicle and take it back home.

Only after I got to RAK did I realize that the visa, a 'white permit' obtained for the grand sum of 3,000 dirhams, came bundled with all manner of restrictions. The result was that I could not even begin to explore business prospects in Dubai, as planned. RAK itself, being one of the emirates without a significant petroleum sector, offered little by way of opportunities for outsiders at that time. A visitor's visa would have served me much better, but I didn't know it then.

The first order of business, I decided, was to change my visa. It turned out that this was a long-drawn-out process, and I would have to wait in RAK while it was accomplished. So, for forty-five interminable days, I cooled my heels in the scrubby desert town, and passed the days by helping out in the jewellery shop.

It was a test of my mental fortitude. I felt trapped in the apartment I shared with the employees of the jewellery business. With no access to a vehicle, and without a valid driving licence, there was no way I could escape to explore the surroundings. In any event, where would I go? There wasn't much to see in the town, and beyond it lay the sands.

The language barrier added to my sense of isolation. I couldn't speak English, Arabic or Hindi. I distinctly recall an Emirati I met at the jewellery store asking why, if I was Indian, I didn't know Hindi!

My palate was unaccustomed to the local fare; I was desperate for good, wholesome Malayalee cuisine. In those days, the restaurant culture did not exist, and unlike today, when supermarkets stock processed foods from across the globe, I couldn't even find any appetizing snacks. In any case, I have always been a fan of home-cooked meals. To keep my mind and hands busy, and to appease my stomach, I began cooking for the first time in my life. Until then, I hadn't so much as stepped into the kitchen. Becoming self-sufficient in the kitchen was a confidence-booster in itself. I thought of what Jolly would say when she would hear about my culinary adventures, and smiled to myself.

It was a stark contrast to my life in India, and even more so to the Gulf lifestyle portrayed in Malayalam films. The 'Gulf Man' always spoke of the prosperity of the UAE and never once mentioned the day-to-day travails suffered by expat workers. So firmly was the narrative of affluence entrenched in the minds of the Keralites back home that it is doubtful whether even Jolly would have bought into my tales of woe!

Difficult though it was, there was no question of going back, because I had volunteered to come. Even as a young man, I never gave in to depression or allowed adverse situations to overwhelm me; that is the advantage of always looking ahead. I focused on building up a knowledge bank for the future. I talked to my hosts, to customers, to just about anyone with whom I could communicate.

After those forty-five days, I moved to Dubai where, by this time, the family network had managed to detect a distant relative. I stayed with him for a week. The city had the high rises, wide roads and gleaming cars that I had hoped to see, but it was very much a work in progress, with vast sandy tracts and the occasional herd of camels.

Dubai's emergence as a port and trading hub of global importance can be traced back to 1902, when H.H. Sheikh Maktoum bin Hasher Al Maktoum, its ruler at the time, abolished all customs duties on imports. The Dubai Creek developed into a thriving centre of commerce, with Indian goods flooding into the city through the port.

As trade volumes exploded, Dubai became the Gulf's hub for re-export to neighbouring ports and inland markets.

Merchants moved en masse to the city, establishing it as the regional headquarters of trade. Indeed, living in the UAE today, one tends to forget that the story of Dubai's economic efflorescence is less than a half-century old. A significant turning point for the city was the dredging of the Dubai Creek in 1960; its widening and deepening created a port accessible to large vessels, thereby increasing trade exponentially. This, in turn, led to a boom in population, and was followed by large-scale infrastructure projects, beginning with the construction of the Al Maktoum bridge which opened in 1963.

Oil was discovered under the sands in 1966, and the UAE itself was formed in 1971, under the leadership of H.H. Sheikh Zayed bin Sultan Al Nahyan, known as the Father of the Nation, and its first president. The dirham was introduced in 1973 under his stewardship. The Jebel Ali Free Zone was inaugurated in 1979, allowing unrestricted import of labour. Its success in attracting foreign investment was to lead to other free zones, setting Dubai on its trajectory to becoming the Hong Kong of the Middle East.

As it turned out, my Gulf odyssey had begun at just the right time, because the UAE in general and Dubai in particular were on the cusp of transformation. The visionary rulers of Dubai were about to launch a massive development and diversification programme that would script an economic miracle and make Dubai a tourism, trading and trans-shipment hub.

Alukkas Arrives in Abu Dhabi

The exigencies of my visa demanded that I go back to India and reapply for a different one. The process entailed some paperwork, but after about six months or so, I was able to secure a business visa. I prepared to return to Dubai. Jolly and my son John Paul, who was a year old by this time, would join me later.

My very first business venture in the UAE was the Hasawi General Trading Company, which was into wholesale trade and small-scale jewellery manufacturing. It didn't do particularly well, but then, my objective in setting it up was not business per se. I merely wanted a platform whereby I could explore the market for jewellery in the UAE, understand the regulatory environment and learn the ropes.

Then, my brother Jos arrived in Dubai. He had come, he said, with a touch of condescension, to introduce me to a builder from Thrissur who was about to launch a construction project in the region. The building industry was taking off in a big way, and it would be good for me to get in on the ground floor of a potentially lucrative business.

I read between the lines. The fact was that Jos and the others were highly sceptical of my ability to run an independent venture overseas, so he had decided to take matters into his own hands. None of my brothers were particularly keen for me to start a jewellery business in the UAE. From the Alukkas point of view, my sole purpose was to secure NRI status and serve as a tax shelter.

I knew perfectly well that Jos saw the proposed partnership as a means to maintain his control over all aspects of the business. I firmly refused the proposal.

'I'm not going to enter into any partnership, for any business. I would rather go back to India than enter into a partnership,' I said.

Jos stayed for three days, but I would not change my mind. He returned to India.

Meanwhile, somebody I knew and trusted, a bank employee, approached me with a request to arrange thirty-three visitor visas through my trading company. This was not an unusual request; NRI-led companies in the Gulf were often asked to arrange visas for Indian nationals. The only curious aspect was the large number of visas—each one cost one thousand dirhams or so in those days, so clearly a lot of money was involved. I agreed in good faith and turned to my sponsor for the necessary paperwork.

At the time, one needed a sponsor to open a business in the UAE. The Arabic term was 'khafeel', someone who would hold a 51 per cent share in the business, albeit without investing any money. The custom was to pay them a fixed remuneration as a sponsorship fee, rather than a share of profits or dividends. It was vital to have a sponsor who was well-connected with various government departments, in order to facilitate approvals and authorizations.

My sponsor fit the bill perfectly: he was Jassim Al Hasawi, a lieutenant colonel with the Ministry of the Interior, and a very cooperative gentleman. I had met him on my first visit to Dubai through a fellow Thrissurian who was then working for the civil defence department. Jassim had agreed to become my 'local', or sponsor, and had never let me down. As always, he was willing to oblige and signed the forms. The visas were duly arranged.

No sooner had all the thirty-three persons I had sponsored landed in Dubai than they vanished into thin air. It turned out that they were illegal migrants. I was in a panic. The colonel was travelling in Europe at the time and I couldn't reach him. Jolly and John Paul were to arrive that very day, so I went to the airport to receive them. I told Jolly what had happened. She was very reassuring, but I couldn't sleep for the next three days. If I was unable to prove that I had not colluded with the illegals, matters could get very serious from a legal standpoint. It was only after my sponsor arrived and sorted out the issue that I was able to relax.

That unfortunate episode apart, I was becoming increasingly restless and dissatisfied, because my ambition to open a jewellery store in the UAE remained unfulfilled. I was running a small-scale wholesale jewellery business, carrying products back and forth in my Toyota Corolla. I had traversed the entire UAE market, acquired first-hand knowledge of the gold trade, and built up a network of contacts. The Gold Souk in Dubai was my stomping ground, and I had learnt the layout of every last gully.

The wholesale business operated on thin margins and payments were often delayed. The volume of business was very low, so for the most part, I felt underemployed. For almost a year, I told myself, I had been marking time in Dubai, doing nothing to further my ambitions.

I wanted to launch a retail business, but my brothers were not ready to take the plunge. A favourite tenet of mine is that one can never be 100 per cent ready for anything, but one should move forward regardless. My brothers, however, repeatedly pointed out that with the Iran–Iraq war still raging, the region was unstable, and therefore, did not merit a substantial investment. In any case, they argued, our two showrooms in Kerala were doing very well and investing in the Gulf would be more likely to create headaches than add value to Alukkas.

Besides, said my brothers, there was always risk in doing business on foreign soil. After all, the sponsor technically owned 51 per cent of the company and could walk away with it at any time. Nor could one rule out the possibility of the regulatory ecosystem becoming adversarial to foreigners overnight.

I decided to go to India and meet with the family in person, with the express purpose of convincing my brothers to let me go ahead. The dynamics within the family had changed by this time. My father was very much on board with my idea, and encouraged me to set up my own venture, but he had gradually withdrawn from the day-to-day running of the jewellery business. When he handed it over to his sons, each of them technically had a one-sixth share, but effectively, Jos and Paul called the shots.

I brought my persuasive skills to bear on the family. I began by pointing out that the timing for a store in the UAE could not be better. The UAE in general and the gold business in particular was poised for spectacular growth, and Alukkas was well placed to take advantage of the opportunity. We were already a well-known brand in Kerala and were bound to find a customer base among the expats in the Gulf, most of whom were Keralites. As for the war, it had been going on for the last seven years, and was bound to come to an end very soon. Finally, in mid-1987, I managed to bring everyone around.

I spoke to an old associate of the family who had set up retail outlets in the UAE some three years earlier: George Varghese, proprietor of Chemmanur Jewellers. As a fellow denizen of Thrissur, he would be inclined to help out a compatriot.

And so it proved. I approached George Varghese, who was some ten years my senior and already had a store in Dubai, for advice and feedback. He was very obliging, considering that I was proposing to become his competitor. But then, the market was large enough to accommodate multiple players, and he already had an established brand, so I did not present much of a threat.

'Joy, you should open an outlet in Abu Dhabi, rather than Dubai,' suggested Varghese.

'Why, Varghese Chettan?' I asked, surprised and perturbed. It was my long-standing ambition to open a store in Dubai, close to the Gold Souk, where I had spent a lot of time while conducting my wholesale jewellery business. In fact, I had taken up accommodation very close to the Gold Souk.

'The gold retail price in Abu Dhabi is significantly higher than in Dubai,' he explained.

I understood the point. Margins in jewellery retail are from two components: first, the profit on making charges, and second, on the price of gold itself. The latter, in the case of Dubai, the centre of the gold trade, would be nil. Abu Dhabi, on the other hand, allowed for a profit on both making charges and gold.

My cousin P.D. Jose entered the picture at this point. He was the son of my maternal uncle, and was to become my longest-serving employee. He had come to the Gulf a few years previously, and had been working with a hose pipe manufacturing company. Despite the fact that he did not have a background in jewellery, he came on board. I sent him to India for four months of training.

Meanwhile, I ran around trying to identify a location—I found a nice space on Hamdan Street—and get the necessary approvals for the store. I stayed at the Delma Hotel Apartment in Abu Dhabi, a very comfortable hostelry. Jolly and John Paul remained in Dubai, while I focused my energies on the job at hand. My family would shift into a furnished apartment at the Delma with me after the store was up and running.

Resources, both in terms of capital and employees, were a constraint, and unravelling the fuzzy mass of regulations was a nightmare. I managed it all single-handedly—finding a sponsor, executing the lease agreement, sorting out issues like labour cards and lack of insurance, as well as banking details, permits and so on. A major drawback was the fact that neither my staff nor I, which by this time included three salesmen—P.D. Jose, Davis P.A. and the late Rafi Vadakkan (a Thrissur native)—knew Arabic. So, we were handicapped when it came to dealing with government documents, which were all in Arabic. A proficiency in the language was a must at the time, as officials did not communicate in any other language.

We addressed the problem by hiring N.P. Antony as a salesman-cum-public relations pointsman. The Alukkas knew his brother quite well, and Jos made it a point to visit their home in Abu Dhabi when he came to the UAE. Antony was working as a turner with an oil piping company there, and had no knowledge of the jewellery industry. I told him that I needed his language skills, and he agreed to help out for a bit. He was inclined to go back to his previous job after a few months, but I persuaded him to stay on. He proved invaluable in interfacing with the local authorities, and arranging work permits, trade licences and so on.

On 1 January 1988, the first Alukkas store outside Kerala opened in Abu Dhabi. The honours were done by Amrita Singh Rathore, wife of Inderjit Singh Rathore, then India's ambassador to the UAE. My older brothers came down for the inauguration; Jolly was there as well. An advertisement in Malayalam in *Gulf News*, one of the more prominent English-language newspapers in the UAE, announced the opening of Alukkas Jewellery, 'Opp: Sheikh Hamdan Centre, Abu Dhabi'. I bought myself a Mercedes-Benz 300 S to mark the occasion.

Running the store was a strenuous job; every second day, I had to make the 150 kilometre run to Dubai to procure jewellery. Owing to capital constraints, I couldn't afford to maintain stock. And credit was not easy to obtain, because although Alukkas was a well-known brand in Kerala, it was virtually unknown in the UAE. As soon as an item—bangles, chains, necklaces, rings or earrings—was sold, I had to dash off to replace it. Most of the jewellery was sourced from Dubai; the rest from India and elsewhere.

On the credit front, George Varghese came to my aid. After the Abu Dhabi showroom opened, I didn't have many products to display. All told, I had perhaps three to four kilos of gold jewellery, not enough to make the store shine. Varghese suggested that I approach a wholesaler by the name of Al Anwar Jewellery for credit. Gratefully accepting his advice, I walked into the office of the proprietor, Ram Popli, at the Gold Centre building in Dubai and put forward my request for jewellery on credit.

'How much do you require, in terms of weight?' Popli asked.

'About ten kilograms,' I replied.

He handed me a calculator. 'Please calculate how much credit ten kilograms of jewellery is worth in Indian rupees.'

I looked at the string of zeroes on the screen silently. Needless to say, he did not give me credit.

Back I went to George Varghese. When I told him the story, he was kind enough to take me to Zumuruda Jewellery, a wholesaler of Iranian origin, where he introduced me and issued a guarantee cheque for ten kilograms of gold. His act of kindness was magnified by the fact that he had no assurance whatsoever that the Alukkas family back in India would make good the money, in the event that I was unable to pay it back. It was a measure of his conviction that I would do well in Abu Dhabi.

As for Al Anwar, many years later, in 2008, when I opened my first store in Mumbai in the upmarket locality of Bandra, I dropped into their office without an appointment and reminded the proprietor of our meeting in the UAE!

In India, we were accustomed to selling kilograms worth of jewellery every day. In Abu Dhabi, we counted our daily sales in grams, which must have been a subject of great derision back home. But, as I repeatedly told myself, it was early days yet.

The Judas Moment

In November 1988, less than a year after the Abu Dhabi outlet opened, the flagship Alukkas store was inaugurated in Dubai. Given that the Abu Dhabi store was doing reasonably but not spectacularly well, why did I hurry to open a second store? Therein lies a tale of betrayal, hurt and a determination to turn adversity into opportunity.

The story began with an advertisement in *Gulf News* in September 1988. By that time, we had been in business in Abu Dhabi for a little over eight months. And the ad in question was aimed directly at us.

'Customers should beware when they buy gold from Abu Dhabi, Abu Dhabi gold price is higher,' read the headline.

It was correct. Certainly, the gold price in Abu Dhabi was higher. On the other hand, if a customer chose to purchase their jewellery in Abu Dhabi rather than make the trip to Dubai, why would anyone have a problem with that? It just didn't make sense that someone wanted to go after my business for no apparent reason.

I had to find out who had put out the advertisement. I got in touch with a gentleman from the ad department of *Gulf News* and learnt the identity of the person behind the offending ad. It turned out to be none other than George Varghese, my adviser and mentor. To me, the blatant attempt to undermine my business felt like a breach of trust. It was my Judas moment.

Clearly, Chemmanur Jewellers had lost out on customer traffic coming from Abu Dhabi. In other words, I was 'blocking' their sales. The fall in sales figures had prompted Varghese to take underhanded action. Why had he encouraged me to open a store there in the first place? Was it because he had not wanted me to set up shop in competition with him in Dubai? Was that why he had generously extended credit to me when no one else would? Ironically, Alukkas had become a competitor anyway, by eroding his Abu Dhabi customer base!

Hurt and angry, I tossed and turned all night, and at five the next morning, I drove from Abu Dhabi to Dubai. I was determined to confront Varghese. I parked outside his store and waited for him to arrive. Fortunately, I had reached well in advance of opening hours, so I had plenty of time to work through my anger.

Once I had cooled down, I began to think more rationally. I asked myself, what do you do when someone draws a line in the sand? Do you erase that line, or do you draw a longer line instead? I decided that the latter was a better course of action. I would not lock horns with Varghese; instead, I would vindicate myself by beating him at his own game.

A strategy clicked into place in my head. I decided, then and there, to open a store in the exact same building as Chemmanur Jewellers. Varghese had chosen to undermine me. I would now turn the tables on him, without making it seem like a direct confrontation. That would be better use of my creativity and energy. My anger and frustration dissipated, and I found myself infused with diamond-hard determination.

Standing outside the building which housed the Chemmanur store—the Gold Central Building of the Dubai Gold Souk in Deira—I made a mental map of its geography. Varghese's outlet was on the mezzanine floor, with a staircase leading up to it. On the ground floor next to the base of the staircase was a Lee Jeans showroom. That, I told myself, is where I will open my jewellery store.

I could see that there were other vacant shops on the ground floor, but this one was uniquely located. It was at the centre point of the main passage, which was open from two sides. The store and its signage would be the first thing that any visitor walking into the Gold Souk would see. Customers heading up to Chemmanur Jewellers would be confronted by the Alukkas showroom even before they stepped onto the staircase.

Other than the Lee Jeans showroom and the vacant spaces, there was a cafeteria, a supermarket, a video cassette library, a stationery store, a shoe store and a small shop selling tailoring materials. All of these were on the ground floor, and would contribute to footfall. Chemmanur's competition, Elite and Vijaya Jewellery, were on the mezzanine floor.

I gathered that only the ground and mezzanine floors were devoted to commercial establishments, whereas the rest of the building was residential, occupied for the most part by expats from Gujarat. Today, the entire building is commercial and is at the heart of the gold trade, with several companies having their offices there.

I made inquiries about the availability of the Lee Jeans showroom. The owner was an Iranian, and he was willing to let it go for the grand sum of 1,00,000 dirhams. This amount, referred to as 'pagdi' in South India and 'key money' in UAE, was basically the premium paid to acquire a good location from an existing tenant. It was a hefty sum, which I later learnt had broken existing records in terms of key money.

That morning, I registered the contract for the shop in my name. In the afternoon, even before the ink was dry on the documents, I met George Varghese and informed him that I was opening a second store, in Dubai. I showed him the advertisement in *Gulf News*, but did not mention that I knew who was behind it. It was only then that I informed my brothers of what I had done. My father, when he heard that I had taken a space in the Gold Souk, was delighted. 'Nannayi' (well done), he told me in Malayalam. This was the first time that my father had voiced his appreciation for a job well done.

My experiences in Abu Dhabi held me in good stead in terms of getting the Dubai store off the ground. On the personal front, Jolly and I were blessed with our first daughter, who was born at Abu Dhabi's Corniche Hospital on 30 August 1988, the day after Jolly's birthday. She was named Mary, after Jolly's mother. I was thirty-two years old at this time—the proprietor of two stores, father of two children and bearer of the Alukkas standard in the UAE.

Rules and regulations were different in each emirate, but I managed to get the approvals in a few months—no mean feat in Dubai. I called upon my sponsor, Jassim Al Hasawi, to inaugurate the showroom. The Dubai store was a calculated risk on my part—a leap of faith, as it were—and it paid off handsomely. I learnt that in brick-and-mortar retail, three things are important: location, location, location. The Dubai showroom stands as an enduring testimony to my innate instinct for ideal locations.

This is not to understate the contributions of my team. Apart from P.D. Jose, Davis P.A. and Antony, who continued to serve as PRO-cum-salesman, as well as our chief liaison with government agencies, there was Thankachan, a young man from Thrissur. He had joined the Alukkas showroom in Calicut as a salesman at twenty-one. Young though he was, he proved a good performer.

I had had my eye on him for a while. On one of my frequent visits to India, I turned to him and said casually, 'Thankachan, are you coming with me?'

He was surprised at first and then, when he realized that it was a serious offer, very excited.

'Yes, sir! I will come!' he declared.

I laughed, charmed by his enthusiasm; he had not stopped to think it over or to consult his parents.

It proved to be a good decision. I arranged for Thankachan's passport, visa and ticket, and he joined the Dubai store. He spoke only Malayalam at the time, which wasn't a serious handicap because most of our customers were from Kerala, but soon picked up English and Hindi on the job.

In those initial years, we all worked very hard, living and breathing Alukkas. I multitasked as manager, proprietor and stand-in salesman. My paternal cousin, P.V. George, was with me in Dubai. Although he was not a regular staffer, he attached himself to me like a shadow during my initial days in Dubai. The staff was small, and they cheerfully put in long hours. I had put them up in the residential accommodation on the upper floors of the Gold Centre, so there was no transit time to and from the store. Life and work melded into a composite whole.

When people talk about work–life balance, I remember those early years. Somehow, despite the long workday, none of us felt pressured. There was no friction between employees, with everyone conscious of working towards a common goal. So absorbed and focused were we, so immune to distraction, that we barely noticed the passage of time. Aware and alert, our actions completely in sync, we effortlessly executed our respective tasks. Duty hours flowed seamlessly into downtime and vice versa. Later, I was to learn that this fluidity between mind and body is termed the 'flow state'.

The Dubai Gold Souk store eventually became our flagship and, of course, our largest revenue earner. It has provided trained staff and capital for expansion and to this day, my employees fondly refer to it as the 'Main Shop'. As for Varghese, he and I continue to maintain a courteous relationship, although he has retired from business and lives in Bengaluru. I do not bear a grudge; if anything, I am grateful to him for having prompted me to take one of the best business decisions of my life.

My parents came to visit me in Dubai, and we had a wonderful time. I took them to see the emirates, and in the midst of all the high-spirited fun, we bonded. It was my father's first trip, and when he went back to Thrissur, I went with him. We sat next to each other on the flight and in the car heading home, with Appan cracking jokes, laughing and discussing all the things he had seen and experienced in the UAE. I had never spent so much one-on-one time with him and felt closer to him than ever before.

Fate was kind enough to give me a few pleasant days with the man who had shaped my character and destiny, before we were parted forever by the implacable fact of death. Even as Alukkas was on the cusp of taking off in the UAE, I received awful news from back home. Appan had fallen gravely ill. I went to Thrissur to see him, and spent many hours by his sick-bed. He had a kidney infection, followed by a heart attack.

On Tuesday, 5 December 1989, at five minutes past midnight, Puthussery Alukka Joseph Varghese closed his eyes for the last time. He was seventy-six. The Dubai showroom downed shutters for two days, out of respect for the man to whom it owed its existence.

In death, as in life, my father remained true to his values. In his final will and testament, he declared that his one-sixth share of the jewellery business was to be spent on charitable works.

I missed him, but my predominant emotion was one of gratitude, for all the love and learnings that I had received from him. Death is a part of the cycle of nature, and I preferred to celebrate the fact that he had lived a long and productive life. I recalled his pride in the success of Alukkas, how his eyes would gleam when it was mentioned, and I made a promise to myself: one day, I would make Alukkas a globally recognized brand.

6

War, and a Golden Age of Peace

-W-

War clouds gathered over the Middle East in the early months of 1990. The Arab world appeared to be on the cusp of an armed conflict. At midnight, on 2 August, the Iraqi invasion of Kuwait began. Some nine hundred kilometres to the south, Dubai was gripped by an air of unease. We went about our business as usual, but an unspoken question remained in the back of our minds: was there a threat to Dubai's security?

In subsequent weeks, refugees from Kuwait began flooding into the emirates. The UAE was sympathetic to Kuwait's travails; its then president, the ruler of Abu Dhabi, H.H. Sheikh Zayed bin Sultan Al Nahyan, arranged accommodation and extended financial support to the displaced Kuwaitis.

I was naturally concerned about the Indian community in Kuwait, and closely followed news reports describing how trade and businesses had been shut down, or fallen prey to looting and vandalism. A mass evacuation began. From August to October, more than 1,70,000 Indians nationals were flown home from Kuwait by the Indian government—a difficult exercise, as the United Nations (UN) had imposed sanctions against Iraq.

The Indian diaspora in Dubai, which had been living here for fifteen to twenty years, began talking about going back to India. I pointed out that Dubai seemed very safe, with no disruption in our day-to-day lives. The airport and other transport services were functioning smoothly. But the atmosphere of uncertainty deepened, and people started leaving for India.

Initially, the war seemed to have a positive impact on the gold trade. This was not unexpected; in times of uncertainty, prices of and demand for gold tend to rise as people see it as a safe investment. As talk of an impending war gained momentum, our sales increased. The Indian expats in the Gulf began putting their savings into gold before leaving for home.

But sales soon dried up, as manufacturers and wholesalers stopped the distribution of jewellery, fearing that they would not be paid if their creditors fled the city. Our jewellery stock rapidly diminished to half, and the store looked vacant. Jewellery traders and retailers began leaving the country. Dubai's Gold Souk became an empty shell.

Our store in Abu Dhabi had closed, as the Hamdan Centre where it was located was to be torn down. I settled with the suppliers; staff salaries, too, were paid in full.

Friends and my immediate family advised me to return home. Economic activities had slowed significantly. Even the thriving textile and garments industry came to a standstill, with wholesalers and manufacturers quitting the UAE.

Finally, I decided to return to India, as I would achieve nothing by staying back.

Besides, I wanted to get my family home. However minimal the risk, I could not expose my children to it. John Paul and Mary were five and two years old, respectively, so I decided to send them back. The Dubai showroom downed shutters, and the inventory was locked in our safe. P.D. Jose and a handful of other staff members, who were convinced that there was no threat to life, remained in the city. Antony was one of them (like Jose, he was to have a long innings with Alukkas). Thankachan, meanwhile, secured a job in the Dubai Duty Free and quit Alukkas, but remained in close touch with us.

On 29 November 1990, the day that the UN authorized military intervention in Kuwait, I left my apartment in the Bur Dubai district, and took a flight to Thiruvananthapuram. Peace would return to the region and business would pick up where it had left off—this was not merely wishful thinking on my part, but a fact-based assessment. Dubai has always benefitted in times of crisis; be it from war-torn Lebanon or Somalia, the erstwhile Soviet Union or post-revolution Iran, wealthy elites converged on Dubai when things became unpleasant at home.

We decided to stay in Calicut with Francis. John Paul was enrolled in kindergarten. I was delighted to see John and Mary finally getting to know their cousins. All the children got along famously, enjoying each other's company and having a great time. Jolly, too, was thrilled to meet all our relatives and spend quality time with them. But I was restless, because I had nothing specific to do in Calicut.

Every day, I scanned the newspapers and watched the news on TV for updates on the war. My brothers weren't particularly concerned about the war, because it did not affect them directly. As usual, they were focused on the business.

P.D. Jose and P.V. George were my main sources of information. They called me on a daily basis. Thousands of soldiers, I was told, were passing through the UAE and the American naval vessel, USS *Portland*, was berthed at Dubai port.

A few weeks later, in January 1991, Operation Desert Storm commenced; TV channels in India and in the UAE began relaying *CNN*, which was covering the war round the clock. By 28 February, it was all over. Kuwait was free and the war had come to an end. I was relieved and so was Jos. He was worried about Alukkas' investment in the UAE, and immediately began asking me, 'When are you going back?'

A week later, I returned to Dubai, which was now under the stewardship of H.H. Sheikh Maktoum bin Rashid Al Maktoum; his father H.H. Sheikh Rashid bin Saeed Al Maktoum had passed away in October 1990.

A New Beginning

An air of optimism pervaded Dubai in the post-war period. In just a month, transport systems normalized and hotels re-opened at full capacity. There was a reverse migration; people returned in hundreds of thousands, so much so that schools had to expand their classrooms to accommodate students. The last US ground troops left the Gulf in June 1991, but the 'globocop' remained a palpable presence in the region, holding out the promise of a lasting peace.

The UAE took advantage of the newfound atmosphere of amity to expand its economy. Dubai, lacking the oil reserves of Abu Dhabi, was an early proponent of diversification. The industrial sector expanded, as did construction and real estate.

The Dubai Creek, an important commercial centre, had served as a magnet for gold traders for decades. A thriving market in precious metals developed adjacent to the Dubai Creek on the Deira side, and came to be known as the Gold Souk (in Arabic, 'souk' means market). It evolved into the largest gold market in the world—a claim that's hard to prove but equally hard to dispute.

The gold and jewellery sector benefitted from the post-war boom. It was dominated by Indians, who had been operating in Dubai since the late 1950s. Tawhid Abdullah, founder of Damas, whose father came to the UAE in 1963, recalls that the term Gold Souk came into popular usage in the 1970s. At the time, he says, Indian jewellers dealt in 21-karat products. A businessman from Gujarat, Devji Purushottam, was the first to introduce 22-karat jewellery to Dubai.

Describing the evolution of the gold trade in the Middle East, Tawhid said Lebanon was the hub for gold jewellery until a civil war erupted in 1975, driving the trade to Kuwait. In 1980, the Kuwaiti government introduced strict hallmarking standards for gold, for which the industry was unprepared. As a result, the industry moved en masse to Dubai, where the government created a conducive policy environment to attract and promote the gold and jewellery sector.

Gradually, jewellers from South India who dealt in 22-karat gold came to dominate that segment of the market. Volumes of 22-karat jewellery surged with the exponential increase in the number of Indian expatriates in the UAE. At the time I came to Dubai, retailers were broadly divided into those who dealt in 18-karat, 21-karat or 22-karat gold jewellery. The gold business was highly fragmented at the time; Alukkas was one among scores of small jewellers.

When I returned to the city on 9 March 1991, I took stock of the situation and decided to make some changes. The Gold Souk had become active again, with most outlets reopening, including Chemmanur and Atlas jewellers. But customers were still scarce. To attract maximum footfall, we needed to differentiate our store from the rest. The Alukkas store was rather large and our inventory was limited, so we had lots of empty space. The old store fit-out relied on dazzling customers with stacks of jewellery, but we had to find alternative modes of display.

I decided to restructure the space to make it more visually appealing. To that end, the jewellery layout became compact and at the same time, more tasteful, thereby improving the ambience and enhancing customer experience. We threw open our doors to customers. To mark a new beginning, we invited the well-known actor, Ramya Krishnan, to light the traditional lamp. Jolly and the children, who had rejoined me in Dubai, were also present.

In the 1990s, our tagline was 'oru panna thookammunpil' (one step ahead), which reflected our values, attitude and approach to all our operations, be it product design, customer service or advertising. We were always open to change, to better ways of doing business. For instance, we introduced computerized billing in 1988, at our Calicut store. The hardware was sourced from Wipro and the software was developed by TACT Private Limited, a Kerala-based entity.

Initially used for purchases, sales and preparing estimates for customers, it had a single-user interface, so the terminal was placed near the cashier and was hooked up to a dot matrix printer. Customers welcomed and were pleased with the computer-generated bills, a practice that gained momentum among other jewellers in a matter of a few years.

The Alukkas group stayed one step ahead by upgrading to a software developed in the 'C' language on the Unix Operating System platform. When we reopened in the Gold Souk, I brought Praveen Theophilus, a computer engineer from TACT Private Limited to Dubai in order to implement an upgraded version of the Unix OS that enabled multiuser interface and added security features. We were the first jeweller in Dubai to have a computerized billing system.

I had taken a conscious decision not to sit at the sales counter, in order to devote my energies to building the business. Looking back, computerization and moving to the back office were two very significant decisions. Proprietors of jewellery stores in the 1990s invariably sat at the cash counter where, in the absence of computers, billing was done manually. It was a vantage point from which they could monitor all the activities in the showroom, while collecting the cash from sales. The practice stemmed from the sheer value of their inventory; they naturally had to keep a close eye on any and all activities.

Typically, the showroom opened only when the proprietor came in. The movement of stock and cash took place under his direct supervision. Even when he left the store for his lunch break or for any other purpose, a member of his family would take charge until he returned. To my mind, confinement to the cash counter also confined his thinking. The necessity of keeping a close watch on the inventory made him too focused on everyday operations to think creatively.

I was determined not to box myself into an operational role. So, the remaining space in the showroom, on the mezzanine floor, was converted into a 500 square foot office. It was shared between three people: an accountant, Antony and I. Eventually, as the team expanded, we would move the office to a larger space on the sixth floor of the Gold Centre.

In my Gold Centre building office, I regularly held meetings with bankers and suppliers—local as well as foreign. During those meetings, I was often the only one smoking, but none of my visitors raised an objection. Then, one day, a foreign supplier dropped in to see me. He seemed a little uncomfortable throughout our meeting, and left my cabin immediately after it was over, only to return a few moments later.

'Joy, this is your workplace,' he said. 'You must ensure proper discipline here. That starts with you. Please stop smoking in your office.'

Without a word, I placed my cigarette in the ashtray. He left without waiting for a response. All through the day, his statement nagged me. That evening, while I was driving back home, I had a cigarette in my hand. I flipped open my packet of cigarettes and found that there were two more inside. And all of a sudden, I took a decision.

I pulled over to the side of the road, and took my last puff. I picked up the packet of cigarettes, and told myself: 'The workplace is just that, a place of work, where everyone must conduct themselves decorously. Self-discipline and ethics ought to be the cornerstones of my character and of my company.' I threw the packet away, as far as I could. With that one gesture, I ended my relationship with tobacco. I had kicked the butt, so to speak. To this day, most people believe that I quit smoking for reasons of health.

The Board Rate System

The initial years of business were very tough. Competition in the jewellery sector was cut-throat. Showrooms in the Gold Souk downed shutters on a regular basis. As mentioned earlier, Alukkas sales were as low as 100 to 200 grams a day (the weight of a gold chain was around 80 grams). The gold price margin was nil, and making charges were limited because of undercutting. So low were the margins that elaborate packaging was ruled out, and we used paper envelopes.

Footfall improved gradually. Thankachan began coming to the store on weekends, to support the staff during rush hour (he is now a senior sales manager at the Dubai Duty Free). Sales escalated to 200–500 grams a day, and continued to improve. In 1992, we returned to Abu Dhabi. Our store opened in the Omar Bin Yousef building on Hamdan Street— precisely the same location as our previous one! Our sponsor in the UAE capital, Ali Saeed Al Ameri, inaugurated the store, and was our first customer.

Sales picked up at our Dubai store, but the profits didn't. From my father, I had learnt that sustainable profits were necessary to continue in business. Often, a lack of profits is discussed only in hindsight, when a business is failing. Actual profits and margins tend to be overlooked when footfall and sales are increasing.

My strong concerns vis-à-vis the sustainability of my business prompted me to look for innovative ways of generating margins. I discussed the issue with my competitor, the late Ramachandran, who was the founder of Atlas Jewellery. We decided to increase the selling price of gold by twenty-five fils per gram. We invited other jewellers, including Chemmanur, to come on board. None of them, however, were willing to increase the sales price of gold, because they were afraid of losing business. Ramachandran and I tried hard to convince them of the importance of margins, but they lacked the courage to change.

Nonetheless, we stuck to our guns, and from early 1993, we started displaying the gold rate in our showrooms. The price of gold at Atlas and Alukkas was higher than the rest of the Gold Souk. To the surprise of our competitors, we did not lose customers as a result. Gradually, over the next few months, other jewellers—including Chemmanur and Damas, then the leading jeweller—hopped onto the bandwagon.

At first, we encountered strong opposition from smaller jewellers, who campaigned against our gold rate, but we persevered. Gradually, traders all over the UAE began quoting our gold rate. We established a working methodology to communicate the gold rate on a daily basis. It was updated based on the international price and had a built-in margin to offset fluctuation. For the first time, jewellers began earning a reasonable margin.

In 1996, the 'Board Rate System' (our term for fixing the gold rate) was taken over by the Dubai Gold and Jewellery Group (DGJG), a non-profit trade body set up to address the concerns of the sector. I introduced a similar system in other countries where we opened stores. The Board Rate has helped industry players achieve sustainability in the long run by assuring jewellers of a consistent profit. It also allowed me the bandwidth to come up with innovative marketing campaigns.

The cooperation within the jewellery retail sector was possible thanks to healthy competition. We fought for market share, but did not actively create hurdles for each other. My competitors regarded me as a peaceable and ethical individual, who saw the advantage in the prosperity of the industry as a whole.

Business saw a steady uptick from 1993, setting the base for future growth. We were selling 500 grams to one kilogram per day. There were two major reasons for this. The first was our aggressive promotional strategy. For example, in 1993, we introduced the 'Go for Gold Bonanza' and the 'Gold Mine' campaign, in which we issued free raffle coupons on a minimum purchase of jewellery. The winners would receive attractive prizes, from gold bars to cars.

Promotions were nothing new; Chemmanur and Atlas held campaigns from time to time. My use of cars, however, was an innovation inspired by Dubai Duty Free. In the jewellery business, it was a first. I tapped into the aspiration for a car shared by many residents of Dubai, and customers responded enthusiastically. The campaign was to prove so successful that we repeated it at least ten times in subsequent years.

Our marketing mediums were radio stations (one in Hindi and the other in Malayalam) and newspapers. The lucky draws were conducted in the presence of government officials, which ensured transparency, and became a big attraction among gold buyers.

Several of the jewellers in the Gold Souk were initially sceptical about my strategy and approached me with the question, 'Do you check your accounts? Are you sure that this kind of promotion is profitable? What is your profit after factoring in the cost of the lucky draw car and other expenses?' They were partially correct; our profits were nothing to write home about, but demand was climbing by the day. We were adding new customers and Alukkas as a brand was getting recognition and attention.

My competitors did not realize that I had a long-term plan to open a chain of stores in the UAE. Once economies of scale had kicked in, the cost of promotions would come down. Eventually, given the success of our campaigns, most of the jewellers launched their own promotions.

The second reason for the growth of our business—and the sector as a whole—was India's economic liberalization. The P.V. Narasimha Rao-led government had come to power in the wake of a serious balance-of-payments crisis. It had been building for a while and finally came to a head, compelling India to shore up forex reserves by pledging gold to the Bank of England. In 1991, the newly elected government, under the aegis of Finance Minister Manmohan Singh, acknowledged the need for expeditious action and embarked on sweeping reforms.

The previous year, the Gold Control Act had been revoked; a tacit acknowledgement that the government's efforts to contain gold smuggling had been singularly unsuccessful. Thereafter, the Non-Resident Indian Scheme (1992) and Special Import Licence Scheme (1994) were introduced, allowing NRIs to carry up to five kilograms of gold into India. As official channels opened up, smuggling declined significantly, although it continues to this day. The bulk of our customers were Indian expats, so the new policies worked to our advantage.

One of my first initiatives was to introduce a uniform for the staff: khaki trousers and a white shirt. The second was the 'straight shift' idea: traditionally, all retail outlets closed from 1 p.m. to 4 p.m., so that the staff could have a long siesta after lunch. The custom, a natural outcome of Dubai's punishingly hot climate, continued even after most spaces in the city were air-conditioned, and therefore comfortable, even during the hottest part of the day. I realized that if we stayed open during the lunch break, we could generate additional business without incurring any cost. We started the practice, which was quickly adopted by the other businesses.

The Dubai Shopping Festival: A Game-Changer

By the mid-1990s, Dubai was positioning itself as a tourist as well as a trade destination. Residents and rulers alike were reimagining the city as a thriving, multicultural, world-class metropolis. Foreign trading communities converged on the emirate, attracted by its business-friendly environment, superior infrastructure, economic opportunities and liberal spirit. Multinationals now felt safe in making substantive investments in the UAE. It was truly the best of times, after the worst of times.

I felt blessed to be in Dubai at the time; doubly so, when my daughter Elsa was born on 31 July 1994. We were now a five-member family, which created a bit of a space crunch in our home! Not that I was there during the day; I was spending increasingly long hours at work, while Jolly held the fort at home.

In 1995, the Dubai government decided to leverage the emirate's many advantages with respect to the gold trade. First, it had the highest standards of purity in the world. At the time, South Asia did not have hallmarking standards, so 'Bought in Dubai' became synonymous with purity and quality. Second, gold prices were low thanks to the government's laissez faire policy. Gold jewellery was 100 per cent duty-free. Third, Dubai offered a mind-boggling variety of wares, with retailers from over 140 nationalities dealing in gold and diamond jewellery in 14-karat, 18-karat, 21-karat, 22-karat and 24-karat.

The result was a seminal initiative known as the Dubai Shopping Festival (DSF), the brainchild of H.H. Sheikh Mohammed bin Rashid, then crown prince of Dubai and the UAE's minister of defence (now vice-president and prime minister of the UAE, and the ruler of Dubai). H.E. Mohammed Al Gergawi, who oversaw the DSF and served as the first festival coordinator general, gave the jewellery industry pride of place. He worked closely with other government agencies, the World Gold Council (WGC) and the gold retailers of Dubai to make it a success.

The role of the WGC bears special mention. It originated with a group of gold mining companies, who came together to develop and serve the gold market worldwide. To that end, the International Gold Corporation (IGC), headquartered in Geneva, was set up in the early 1980s. The late André Bisang, a Swiss national and the Dubai representative of the Federation of the Swiss Watch Industry, was convinced of the emirate's potential with regard to the gold trade. He was instrumental in persuading the IGC to open an office in Dubai.

The organization was renamed the World Gold Council in 1987, and under the leadership of its first global CEO, E.M. Hood, its presence and activities expanded. Bisang, who was the WGC's Middle East regional head, expanded its operations to India, one of the largest jewellery markets in the world. Pathi Devraj became the first country manager.

At first, the WGC limited itself to creating awareness about gold as an investment as well as an adornment, largely through the media. Madco Gulf was retained as their marketing and creative agency. The account was handled by people I knew: Ravi Prasad and Renjith C.P. Both had a thorough knowledge of the gold industry. Pathi Devraj rejoined the WGC's Dubai team in 1995, under the aegis of the regional CEO, Rolf W. Schneebeli.

In the runup to the first DSF, Al Gergawi asked the WGC to come up with innovative ideas for promoting the gold industry, and ensuring the cooperation of jewellery traders. Pathi's observation was that Dubai had 'offered its best to most of us, and now it is our turn to give back by supporting the DSF initiative'.

The WGC initiated a meeting of the main retailers, among them Tawhid, Ramachandran and me. At the Dubai Chamber of Commerce, we were introduced to the concept of the DSF. As word spread across the industry, the WGC convened a large gathering of jewellers, at which Pathi described the importance of the DSF and its potential benefits. The idea of a raffle as a promotional tactic was shared. Jewellers would purchase raffle coupons from the DSF and pass them on to customers who bought 300 dirhams worth of jewellery—the grand prize being one kilogram of gold every day. The proceeds from the sale of coupons would go towards a marketing campaign and the prize. The idea found wide acceptance among the retailers.

H. E. Mohamed Alabbar, founding director general of the Dubai Economic Department (DED), realized that conducting a large-scale promotional campaign would require close coordination with jewellery retailers. The WGC figured this would be best accomplished through a trade body. That's how the Dubai Gold and Jewellery Group (DGJG)—which eventually took over the Board Rate System, as mentioned earlier—was initially set up with Tawfiq Abdullah, brother of Tawhid, as its first chairman.

The WGC supported the first DSF financially, and also provided guidance on marketing. Through these and other efforts, it had a transformative impact on the gold trade in the region. Dubai became known for its impeccable standards of gold purity, exquisite designs and fair-trade practices. It created an ecosystem for jewellers to grow while allowing customers to benefit from the healthy competition.

Under Hood, the WGC began propagating Dubai as the 'City of Gold', a tagline the city has earned and retained to this day. Alukkas had the best sales of any jewellery retailer in the city, which meant that we bought the highest number of lucky draw coupons from the DSF, and passed them on to our customers. Naturally, this gave us the best odds of having winning customers. Sure enough, we had the highest number of winners. The newspapers published their names and I displayed their photographs at the store. I removed them later, at the instance of other retailers. Word got around that Alukkas was a 'lucky store'; so much so that smaller jewellers in the Gold Souk began buying gold from Alukkas during the DSF.

When subsequent DSFs were held, we found that our customer base had increased substantially.

On one particular day during the DSF, we sold twenty-eight kilograms of gold, virtually half the amount we had in stock. I organized a party that day. The incident went a long way in convincing all the stakeholders in the DSF of its immense potential, and engendered my ambition to have a second showroom in the Gold Souk.

The DSF became an institution in itself, and contributed significantly in branding Dubai as the City of Gold. For the jewellery industry, the key learning was the benefit of participating in a unified marketing activity. From then on, retailers started promoting themselves independently, just as I had been doing all along.

The visionary government of Dubai spared no effort to attract tourists and shoppers from across the world. A big step forward for tourism and commerce was the establishment of the Department of Tourism Commerce Marketing (DTCM) in 1997. The WGC, meanwhile, lobbied strenuously with the government for a conducive policy environment. They also worked with the jewellery industry on a series of promotional events, and dovetailed the City of Gold brand with high-profile sporting events such as horse-racing and golf.

Meanwhile, the DGJG has gone from strength to strength, and we now have over 400 members. We also organize sector-wide retail campaigns, including the DSF draw, under the aegis of the newly established Dubai Economy and Tourism department. In addition, we conduct training workshops aimed at developing skills such as diamond-grading and salesmanship.

Self-regulation has ensured that our quality standards continue to be the highest in the world.

The Trust Factor

Back in India, Alukkas was doing well. Francis had mooted the idea of a third showroom in Chennai, after Thrissur and Calicut, in 1990. He felt it was important to establish the Alukkas brand outside Kerala, and Tamil Nadu has a large appetite for gold jewellery. I had spent a week helping with the inauguration of the store, as the Gulf War was on at the time. Unfortunately, the store failed, owing to a combination of factors. The location was not advantageous and Alukkas did not enjoy brand recall outside Kerala. We closed the store in a matter of months (I was back in Dubai by then). However, by 1994, Alukkas had added three more showrooms, one additional store each in existing markets (that is, Thrissur and Calicut) and a third in the city of Kochi, on the commercial high street of MG Road. All these stores were thriving.

In 1994, we redesigned the Alukkas logo. The old logo, with its relatively inconspicuous diamond-in-diamond graphic, coupled with an unimaginative font, did nothing to enhance our brand. The new one, featuring a line-sketch of a bejewelled woman and a mix of two fonts, was eye-catching and captured the changing ethos of womanhood: confidence and an attitude of 'if you've got it, flaunt it'. Simultaneously traditional and modern, the logo was created by Chrysalis Advertising in Kerala.

The new logo was adopted by all the Alukkas stores in India and the UAE, and the signage was changed accordingly.

By this time, Alukkas was well-established and enjoyed considerable brand recall in the UAE. Our customers were mostly from Kerala, where we had five stores. We leveraged that fact to position ourselves as a jewellery chain, which added to our brand equity.

I also deployed video cassettes of popular Malayalam films to promote our brand. From the early 1990s, Video Home System (VHS) tapes—basically, audio–visual recordings on magnetic cassette tapes—had become popular among consumers. Full-length movies could be recorded and played on video cassette recorders (VCRs). Indian expatriates in the Gulf who visited their homes in Kerala invariably carried VHS tapes of films back with them. The very first Alukkas advertisement was an insert in one of these films. In a short span of time, Alukkas became a household name. However, my ambition to expand into every corner of the GCC remained unfulfilled, as my brothers were still reluctant to invest in the UAE. Perhaps they saw limited potential in the Gulf—or in me!

Around 1997, owing to events within the family (described in the next chapter), my brothers finally acquiesced to my long-held ambition of opening new stores, but with a caveat. 'Joy, you can open more shops if you want, but we will not be able to fund it from our Kerala business. If you can manage capital from the UAE, you can go ahead,' they said.

By this time, we had four stores in the UAE. I knew that further expansion would not be supported by the family business. Where would I find the money? Financial institutions regarded jewellers as a risky proposition. For one thing, the quantum of investment involved was huge, as much as ten to fifteen million dirhams. For another, jewellery retail was highly fragmented and unorganized, with a mobile inventory that could be easily transported. So, banks did not see us as credit-worthy.

We were heavily dependent on suppliers' credit, and bought jewellery on fifteen to thirty days' credit. The cash flow from sales went towards paying the supplier, who would then give us another consignment. The circular flow continued, but managing working capital and meeting suppliers' payments was a bit of a walk on a tightrope.

At this stage, an important landmark in my journey occurred when the Bahrain-based bullion wholesaler Yusuf Nunu approached me for help.

'Mr Joy, I want to open an office in the Gold Centre building. Can you arrange an introduction with the management?' he asked.

'Certainly, no problem,' I said.

I provided a reference and helped him find a suitable space. He began trading in gold bullion and kept in touch with me.

One day, he told me that I ought to purchase my gold requirements from his company. The credit norm for bullion at that time was one day; that is, the buyer would purchase gold against a cheque that was post-dated by a day.

Like most jewellers, I maintain an unfixed or open price position with bullion suppliers, so as to hedge against possible gold price fluctuation. In effect, you pay the price prevailing on the day of settlement.

In 1997, the gold price started to fluctuate erratically. At one stage, gold prices were following an upward trend, and I was suffering losses as a result. So, I sent Nunu a message, asking him to 'fix' the entire value of gold I had received from him. The amount ran into millions of dirhams. But gold is a capricious entity, and in a matter of days, the price crashed and came back to previous levels. I could have kicked myself—by fixing my position at a higher price, I had incurred substantial losses.

When the account statement arrived from Nunu's office, I ran my eye over it, and was dumbfounded. It showed that I had not fixed (bought) any gold position. I called his office to point out the error, and was told: 'Please come and receive your margin money. It has been lying with us.' It turned out that Nunu had forgotten to fix my position with his counterparty bank when the gold price was high. So, I now had to pay a much lower rate. I had benefitted from Nunu's forgetfulness! As he later recalled: 'Considering the margin money ran into millions, if it had been someone else, we would have never noticed such grave discrepancies.'

He also told me, 'You should take advantage of the current low price and fix your gold.' Our professional and personal relationship deepened after this incident, based on mutual trust. When I shared my plan to open an Alukkas outlet in Qatar with him, Nunu said: 'Joy, buy gold only from me. From now on, I want to be your exclusive supplier.'

I laughed and agreed, but asked with a smile, 'how much credit will you give me?'

'How much do you want?'

'I need one hundred kilograms!'

'No problem!' he replied, smiling right back at me.

For Nunu to provide me with a large value of goods on credit, without collateral or paperwork of any kind, was a windfall. The one hundred kilograms later increased to two hundred and then three hundred kilograms. I was able to achieve my ambition of opening new stores in the UAE, Qatar and Oman without the benefit of large capital (Jos was still refusing to commit funds for my ventures in the Gulf).

In 1996, Alukkas opened a showroom at the Gold Centre in Sharjah. Among the dignitaries present was H.E. Sheikh Faisal Khalid Sultan Al Qasimi, a member of the ruling family and chairman of the Al Qasimi Group. The following year, we inaugurated our second showroom at the Dubai Gold Souk.

The roll-out of new stores continued in 1998 and 1999. We opened our first store outside the UAE in Doha (Qatar) in 1998. The following year, we threw open the doors of our showroom in Ruwi (Oman). We also inaugurated two more in Sharjah, followed by a third one in Dubai, at the Karama Centre. By the end of the millennium, Alukkas was a visible presence in the Gulf, with ten showrooms spread across the region.

Needless to say, I regard Yusuf Nunu as a major reason for the growth of Alukkas, and I visit him in Bahrain when I can.

The overall increase in the number of stores helped to leverage economies of scale. To put it simply, fixed expenses do not grow in proportion to variable expenses, and this operating leverage allows enhanced profits. The 'virtuous cycle' enabled us to go in for high-profile promotional campaigns, which went a long way in building our image. As the brand rapidly gained acceptance, the scope for sales of premium products expanded. I deployed the Alukkas network back home to import the Indian collection of jewellery to Dubai. It was the beginning of organized jewellery retail in the Gulf.

My staff certainly contributed to Alukkas' growth trajectory. At one stage, P.D. Jose had single-handedly managed the store, while doing the accounts and handling procurement. All of them were deeply invested in the success of our venture, and felt a sense of pride that it was doing well.

Antony continued to serve as our PRO, and helped in staging many of our events. His ability to speak and read Arabic was invaluable in keeping customers happy. He called me 'brother' and although he was older than me, accorded me respect and genuine affection. I found out that he did not have a driving licence, so I encouraged him to learn how to drive. For someone in public relations, I pointed out, it was a valuable skill to have. He eventually got his driving licence, and the very next week, I gifted him a Toyota car. He left the UAE in 2005, to join our corporate office in Ernakulum, Kerala, as manager.

In 1999, Dubai made a big splash in the global media by creating the world's longest gold chain, measuring 3.7 kilometres, or four-and-a-half times the height of the Burj Khalifa. As many as 360 jewellers came together to craft it, but Alukkas was the biggest contributor. We accounted for 1.009 kilometres of the length, and this was booked by 1,680 customers. Taking advantage of the promotional opportunity, we published an advertisement in *Gulf News* titled 'Alukkas Golden Kilometre', naming every one of the customers.

That year, we also held the 'Alukkas Millennium Nite', a mega-event featuring a galaxy of film stars from South India. It was held at venues across the Gulf, and made a big impression on the Indian expat community.

At the dawn of the new millennium, Alukkas shone brightly in two contrasting geographies: the sands of the Gulf and the greenscape of Kerala. In the space of little more than a decade, our Gulf operations had achieved a turnover of one hundred million dollars, and we looked forward to a radiant future.

I was confident, but as I had already learnt, the path to success rarely runs smooth. Even as we launched into a phase of aggressive growth in the UAE from 2000, momentous events were taking place back home.

7

A House Divided

In the winter of 2002, the five Alukkas brothers—Jos, Paul, Francis, Anto and I—gathered at the Alukkas Hotel in Thrissur. The atmosphere was one of palpable tension. On the table and up for grabs were the family's real estate holdings in Kerala. All of them were to be auctioned off among the brothers. Both Jos and I were determined to win.

Jos looked grim, and the others were visibly anxious. I felt relaxed, but resolute. I was going to pull out all the stops to emerge as the victor.

The real estate assets included some minor landholdings, a few buildings, a large stretch of land in Puzhakkal, the Alukkas Hospital, the Alukkas Gardens and the hotel in which we were sitting.

Jos had brought us to this juncture, but the auction had been my idea. It was a defining moment in our family saga. The events that led up to it had begun four years ago, in 1996, when Paul declared that he wanted to chart his own path, and hive off one of the family stores into an independent entity.

Paul and Jos had been at loggerheads. They were very different in terms of their character and roles in the business: Jos was the face of Alukkas in Kerala, whereas Paul worked quietly behind the scenes. Disagreements between them got to the point where Paul decided he was better off on his own. Eventually, an understanding was reached whereby Paul got the Kochi store, which he had been managing, along with all the store inventory, as his share of the business.

A year later, Anto also expressed a desire to run an independent jewellery business. Like Paul, he was excellent at managing the store, a fact acknowledged within the family. He was good with numbers, and was diligent in reconciling accounts at the end of each day—by no means a simple or easy job, as any jeweller knows. But he, too, was uncomfortable being under Jos' thumb. Having given in to Paul, Jos had no choice but to agree. Anto was given one of the two stores in Thrissur, along with the inventory, as his share of the business.

I think Paul and Anto believed that without their managerial skills, the family business would suffer. Both were convinced that it was them, and not Jos, Francis or me, who had contributed the most to Alukkas. After all, they saw themselves as playing a hands-on role, sitting in their stores all day and manning the cash counters. Neither Jos nor I did that. We left the mundane tasks to the staff and focused on promotions, ideating, networking and deal-making. I have always believed that while the minutiae of running an enterprise are important, growing the business means taking a big-picture view. Time has proved me right.

Personally, I would have preferred to avoid the splits. On the other hand, the family partition was an eye-opener for Jos, and as a result, he began slackening his hold on the reins. I took advantage of that. He had been unwilling to allow me to open new stores in the Gulf, but after the partitions of 1996 and 1997, he became amenable to such requests. I was allowed to open more stores, provided I could find funding for them.

The three remaining shareholders in the family business—Jos, Francis and I—had collectively decided not to talk about another partition, at least for some time. But hushed conversations about another anticipated partition were already taking place among our employees. It was a tricky phase for the family business in India, with the Alukkas brothers pulling in different directions. The resulting chaos naturally impacted our employees, some of whom were contemplating resigning. Among them was Justin Sunny, who had been keen on a long-term career with the brand. During one of my visits to India, I asked him whether he would be interested in joining me in the Gulf. He quickly assented.

The business was doing well, both in the Gulf and Kerala, but the two consecutive partitions had taken a toll, in terms of time and energy. Until that point, Jos, Francis and I had an equal share in our business and profits. However, Jos now insisted that his children should get a share of the profit in the business, because they had joined the business and were involved full-time. This was patently unreasonable and illogical, but the last thing we wanted was a fight with Jos. So, I suggested a profit-sharing arrangement in the ratio of 40:30:30 between Jos, Francis and me respectively.

Then, in 2000, Jos came up with a proposal for the third and final partition of the Alukkas holdings. Francis and I were more than willing, because with Jos' children playing an active role, a parting of ways seemed inevitable. Where there had been three, there were now six. The Gen Next brigade naturally had its own opinions and attitudes regarding the running of the business, so Francis and I thought it best for the three of us to separate. Discussions began in 2000, mainly over the telephone. They were cordial for the most part.

A Disappointment

The proposals for the division of assets went back and forth. We had fifteen stores in the Gulf at the time, as well as six in India. I suggested a three-way split in the Gulf, with each brother getting five stores. Obviously, I wanted a share in the Indian stores as well. In particular, I had my eye on the showroom in Thiruvananthapuram, which was to open shortly and was a prestigious property.

Besides, like every Gulf expatriate, I wanted to have a home in Kerala! All my brothers had their homes there, and at that point, I did not imagine staying in Dubai permanently. The majority of Indian migrants in the Gulf wanted to return home after a few years of working there, and I was no different.

In particular, I missed the rain. Dubai gets very little rainfall as compared to Thrissur. There are barely any rainy days, whereas in Thrissur, it rains for several months of the year.

I also missed having a traditional Kerala-style house. In Dubai, we lived in an apartment (it was only in 2001 that we would move into a villa). So, when Alukkas'

Thiruvananthapuram project was announced in 1999, I was hopeful that it could become my home base, so to speak.

I was familiar with the city, because until Kochi acquired an international airport of its own in 1999, we travelled to the UAE from Thiruvananthapuram. Getting there from Thrissur involved a one-day trip with multiple stopovers. I was in and out of India so often that I became well-acquainted with the state capital.

While our store was being constructed, I made frequent visits to Thiruvananthapuram, and was actively involved in the fit-out and design. Even if I do say so myself, the end result was exquisite, with a stunning window display and charming back wall units.

I have always had a penchant for architecture and store design. The aesthetics of the showroom are important to me, particularly the lighting. A white light, or a combination of warm and white light, brings out the brilliance of diamond jewellery. I also take note of the placement of lights, and the intensity. In the large format stores in India, I was looking to experiment with the tried-and-tested designs used in Dubai.

All three of us were very sure of the business potential of the store. Initially, my brothers gave me to understand that they were willing to allot it to me, but later, Jos had second thoughts. Clearly, he knew the showroom was a potential money spinner and wanted it for himself. When the project was nearing completion, he told me: 'Joy, I want the Thiruvananthapuram shop.'

I was shocked. 'But brother, you promised the Thiruvananthapuram shop to me, and I have been working on the store for the past one year. I don't have a place or a piece of land in India; I have been living as a migrant in a foreign land for the last fifteen years; my children need an identity in India,' I expostulated.

We had hit our first roadblock, and the discussions dragged on for a while. At first, we argued over it, but he was adamant. Between Jos and Francis, they decided to keep all the shops in India. 'We don't know the business over there, we don't know what (the exchange rate of the) dirham is and what the system is over there,' they told me. 'The UAE stores are yours; we will divide the shops in India.'

I finally decided not to press the issue. It was obvious they wanted to keep the stores in India as these were far more lucrative. At that time, the showrooms in Kerala were racking up ten times more sales than those in the UAE, with daily sales in excess of eight to ten kilograms per store. Besides, the UAE was unfamiliar terrain for them; they had no idea how the gold business was conducted in the Middle East. So, it suited them to hand over the overseas operations entirely to me.

I found my brothers' myopia vis-à-vis the market in the UAE quite baffling. Dubai had already positioned itself as the City of Gold. Its visionary rulers had gone a step further and envisaged the city as a global economic hub along the lines of a London or New York, with world-class infrastructure, evolving to meet the burgeoning needs of global customers. The world's most luxurious hotel, the Burj Al Arab, was ready, and ambitious projects like the Palm Jumeirah had been announced. A reluctance to jump out of their comfort zone and into a new territory was natural, but the fact was that I had already done the groundwork and established a strong branch network for Alukkas.

By now, I was in a hurry to wrap up the partition and was prepared to accept whatever I was being offered. I eagerly anticipated my imminent freedom, and the possibilities it offered. The prospect of being accountable to no one but myself was thrilling.

Once I had agreed that Jos would have the Thiruvananthapuram store, the discussions on the division of assets proceeded smoothly and all the settlements were finalized within the year. Just as we were ready to draw up the paperwork for the agreement, Jos began to dilly-dally. When I asked him to expedite the matter, he said, 'Okay, we will settle the whole thing after a month.' A month passed. Francis and I broached the subject once again, only to be told that we would have to wait for another three months.

I realized that Jos was dragging his feet over the partition so that he could bill the cost of opening the Thiruvananthapuram store to the family business. If the partition took place before the showroom opened, he would have to bear the expenses, and he had no intention of doing that.

At the end of 2000, he opened the showroom. I was relieved, because we could finally move ahead. Jos then bowled another googly. He insisted that the business should be divided in the ratio of 40:30:30 between him, Francis and me, rather than a one-third share for each of us.

We decided to evaluate and divide the assets and liabilities of our joint business in Dubai and India, with 31 May 2001 as the cut-off date. The gold inventory was calculated and the value fixed based on the price on that day; all other assets and liabilities were also assessed accordingly.

All the formalities were completed on the appointed date. In hindsight, the partition was not very complicated. Jos got his store (at family expense) in Thiruvananthapuram, as well as those in Perinthalmanna and Thrissur, while Francis got the two showrooms in Kozhikode and the one in Kannur. I got all the stores in the Gulf. I had always kept a close eye on certain employees, who had worked with the group during its initial phase of growth and demonstrated proactiveness in learning different aspects of the business; I insisted they should stay on with me.

As mentioned earlier, Appan's will had divided his assets into six parts, five to his sons and the remaining portion to be divided between his daughters and various charities. For instance, the 'tharavadu' or ancestral house in Thrissur, as well as the umbrella unit, was left to my sisters. The proceeds were to be divided equally between them.

Then came the question of dividing the real estate assets. Some were common properties, whereas others were already occupied by my brothers and their families. By mutual agreement, it was decided that whoever was in possession of the premises would keep them. Naturally, that left me out, as I did not live in India.

Jos kept his home in Thrissur and Francis kept his in Kozhikode. Anto received an acre of land to construct a house. Paul, too, was awarded land in Ernakulam. I received gold inventory equivalent to their portions. I was conscious of the fact that after the division, I could not claim ownership of even a single square yard of Indian soil!

Appan, in his will, had also earmarked some money that was to be handed over to his and Amma's siblings.

Mangalya Mela and a Clash

In memory of Appan, I decided to organize the Mangalya Mela. The idea was to extend financial assistance to eligible bachelors from underprivileged backgrounds. I kept aside funds towards all the expenses for the mass wedding, and launched the campaign in October 2001. We placed advertisements in newspapers seeking applications from eligible young women. Out of the 20,000 who applied, 7,953 were shortlisted. Selecting 101 couples was a daunting task. Several committees were set up for the smooth conduct of the event.

Initially, I had chosen Kochi as the venue for the Mela. Although the event had been announced in Dubai, it attracted a great deal of attention in Kerala. Naturally, many of the inquiries were directed at Jos, who was the face of Alukkas in Kerala. Jos came to Dubai and requested me to change the venue to Thrissur. I was aware that my brother, a natural-born extrovert, had built up a wide network of influential contacts in Thrissur, who could help in facilitating arrangements for the Mela. So, I acceded to his request, and the preparations went forward.

The Mela was slated to take place in February 2002. Each bride was to receive eighty grams of gold jewellery, a bridal saree or dress, a bridal kit and ten thousand rupees cash. The event was inaugurated by my mother, and attended by around fifty thousand people, including prominent politicians, cultural leaders and artistes.

The wedding ceremonies took place in accordance with the customs of the community to which the bride and groom belonged, at a church, mosque or temple. Two representatives from Alukkas attended the wedding(s). A grand reception was held at the Thrissur Pooram grounds on 17 February 2002.

Francis, looking at the mounting expenses, chose to pay a small share of the total amount. I approached Jos to ask for his contribution; he flat-out refused to pay. 'I helped you organize the event, since you don't know anything,' he snapped. 'You don't know business, you don't know income tax, you don't know the Kerala market, so how did you imagine that you could organize such a big event?'

Shocked at his outburst, I reminded him that I had moved the event to Thrissur at his request.

'Yes, but I was the one who helped you organize it,' he shot back, and then launched into a tirade against me.

I was extremely angry by now, but held back, as I did not want to harangue my eldest brother. 'If I don't know the business, I suppose you will not mind if I start an outlet in Kerala?'

'I have no problems,' he said in a retaliatory tone. 'Open wherever you want.'

That episode was a turning point in my life; it engendered a steely determination to prove myself.

So it was that some weeks later, when the family gathered to carry out the last of my father's wishes and distribute his share of wealth among Appan and Amma's siblings, I announced that I was going to open a showroom in Kerala.

'Go to Kottayam or Kollam as there are no Alukkas stores there and you will not have any competition,' Jos said sarcastically.

On the following day, I selected the location for my head office in Kochi. I wanted an experienced individual from within the group to manage the office, so I chose George T.A., who had been with Alukkas Jewellery India for seven years. He had a thorough understanding of the gold industry, and in 1997, had undergone training in polished diamond grading at the Indian Diamond Institute (IDI) in Surat.

My office in India opened in April 2002, in the Kurian Towers at Kochi. It was to serve as my headquarters in India. My brothers, who had been keeping a close eye on my activities, asked: 'You're a jeweller, why do you need an office?' The concept of an office was alien to them, as all their business was conducted out of their showrooms.

Before setting up the office, I approached Venugopal, a chartered accountant well known to the family, to incorporate a company for me, under the name 'Alukkas Jewellery International'. He was intrigued, because a standalone jewellery store did not call for setting up a company; a proprietary or a partnership firm would have sufficed. So, I shared my vision with him. 'I need a company and I want to get it listed in ten years,' I said.

In those days, Venugopal sat in a shabby office in a decrepit building. I visited him there, and told him, 'You are a senior CA, well-known and highly respected. Please excuse me for saying it, but this office is not worthy of a person of your stature. You should shift to a better location that is more suitable for you.' Not only did Venugopal find a new office, but he invited me to inaugurate it!

Our relationship deepened and we grew to like each other very much. He liked the fact that I thought ahead, and appreciated my perfectionism. For instance, I have always

PUTHUSSERY
ALUKKA JOSEPH VARGHESE
(1913–1989)

ELIYA
VARGHESE
(1919–2002)

▲ The visionary leader (Appan) and the strongest woman (Amma) I knew.

▲ Family picture taken circa 1965. Back row from left: Philomina, Lucy, Rosily, Elsi, Jos, Mary, Kochuthresya, Jacintha. Front row from left: I, Anto, Appan & Amma, in between are Paul and Reena, standing on right of Amma are Clara and Francis. Amma was expecting Pauly at the time.

▲ Around the age of 16, I started assisting my father. Work became my play as well as a training ground.

▲ I received my first Holy Communion at the age of Nine. The ceremony was held at St. Joseph School Church, Thrissur (then called Trichur).

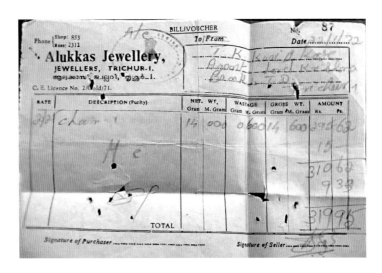

▲ Appan secured the licence issued by the Central Excise and Customs with great effort. A manual bill dated 22 January 1972 bearing C.E. Licence No: 2/Gold/71 from Alukkas Jewellery, Trichur.

▲ With Jolly on our wedding day, 16 September 1984, at St. Joseph's Church, Kuriachira, Kerala. My new bride in her wedding finery, looking radiant.

▲ Jolly and I with our first-born, John Paul, in 1986, shortly before my first trip to the UAE.

▲ The very first visa stamp on my passport in the summer of 1986, an enduring reminder of my forty-five-day ordeal in Ras Al-Khaimah, UAE. I had arrived here with just two changes of clothes and a handful of dirhams.

▲ At the office of the Hasawi General Trading Company, dealing in the wholesale trade of jewellery. This was my first business venture in the UAE (1987). With my office associates P.D. Jose (on the left) and Davis (to the right).

◀ The inauguration of our first store in the Gulf, at Hamdan Street in Abu Dhabi, on 1 January 1988, with Amrita Singh Rathore, wife of Inderjit Singh Rathore (then India's ambassador to the UAE), doing the honours.

▼ The reopening of the Alukkas store in the Dubai Gold Souk post the Gulf War and massive renovations, on 4 October 1991. To date, the store is fondly referred to as the 'main shop' by my staff.

◀ Multitasking as manager, proprietor and stand-in salesman in the initial years of the Alukkas store in Dubai's Gold Souk.

▲ We introduced the first-ever computerized billing system in Dubai, based on the Unix OS with a multiuser interface and security features.

▲ The 1994 advertisement announcing our 'straight shift' policy, whereby we became the first retail outlet in Dubai to work through the traditional 1 p.m. to 4 p.m. lunch-and-siesta break.

◀ Rolf W. Schneebeli, the then CEO of the World Gold Council, inaugurates Alukkas' second showroom at Dubai's Gold Souk on 12 March 1997.

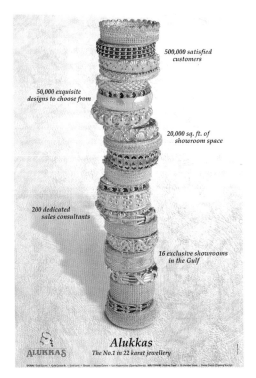

▲ No. 1: Our iconic 'tower of gold' advertisement, with the stack of bangles representing the numeral '1' and symbolizing Alukkas to be the top 22-karat jeweller.

▲ The Alukkas advertisement announcing our promotional campaign, circa 2000. I was a great votary of car promotions because of their mass appeal. If someone offered two cars, I would offer twenty-two cars.

▲ We became the first jeweller to introduce the use of 'purity analyser' or X-ray Fluorescence Spectrometer in the Gulf, for accurate assessment of gold purity in under five minutes.

◀ Our advertisement announcing the Alukkas–World Gold Council 'One World Coin' marking the 'One World, One Family, One Festival' theme of the Dubai Shopping Festival 2001.

Advertisement of the game-changing Rolls Royce campaign (17 June to 13 October 2001) that boosted es and enhanced our brand presence in the Gulf.

▲ Khalid Al Hajiri of Dubai's Department of Economic Development conducting the Rolls Royce raffle draw on 21 October 2001 and holding up the name of the winner. To his right is Yusuff Ali M.A., chairman and managing director of the Lulu Group and our UAE sponsor Jassim Al Hasawi.

▲ The Mangalya Mela organized by Alukkas in Thrissur (February 2002) held in remembrance of late Appan.

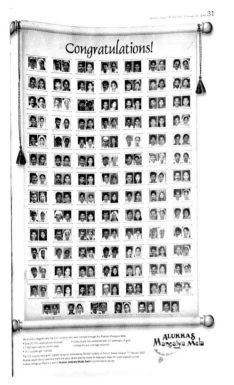

▲ The Alukkas' Mangalya Mela advertisement featuring the shortlisted couples who tied the knot at the event.

▲ Amma inaugurating the office of Alukkas Jewellery International at Kochi's Kurian Towers, marking my first independent foray into India, in April 2002.

▲ Bryan Parker, erstwhile managing director of the World Gold Council, inaugurating my first store in India at the Muthoot building on Kottyam's T.B. Road, Kerala, in 2002. In attendance—my four brothers and UAE sponsor Jassim Al Hasawi.

▲ The 2003 ad depicting the transition of Alukkas to 'alukkas'—an attempt to differentiate my brand and my enterprise.

◀ Bollywood superstar Shah Rukh Khan launching the Alukkas Golden Reward card —the first-ever loyalty programme in the jewellery industry—in Dubai in 2004.

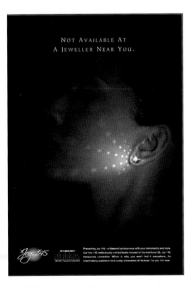

▲ The 2004 ad launching the 'Joy 145' collection of exclusive diamonds, when they were not part of any jeweller's main production line.

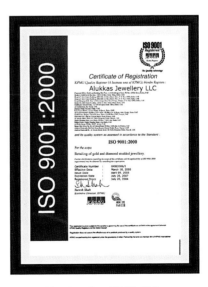

▲ Alukkas Jewellery LLC's ISO 9001:2000 (Quality Management System) certificate of 2004, first awarded to any jeweller in the Middle East.

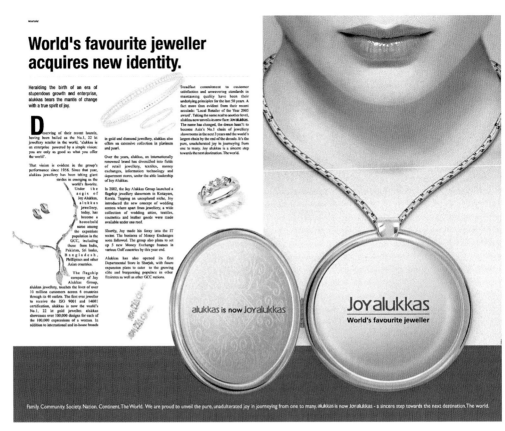

The 2005 newspaper ad announcing the transition of 'alukkas' to 'Joyalukkas' and positioning ourselves as the 'World's Favourite Jeweller'.

'One Woman, 100,000 Expressions': Our very first international campaign, featuring actor-model Chitrangada Singh. The campaign appealed to the masses.

▲ Our first money exchange in Burdubai, UAE, being inaugurated by the then Consul General of India to the UAE, Y.K. Sinha, in 2006.

▲ The inauguration of our first showroom in the UK (14 September 2006) on London's Green Street, with Sir Robin Wales, then Mayor of Newham, and Bollywood actor Bhumika Chawla doing the honours.

▲ Having an aircraft at my disposal allows me to visit existing stores and scout sites for new stores in multiple cities in a day. With my first aircraft, a Vulcanair P.68C Turbo with a propeller engine, purchased in 2006.

▲ The Coca-Cola label used in its 2007 UTC Promo Campaign, held in association with Joyalukkas, describing the prizes to be won—5,000 gold coins and three diamond necklaces, all furnished by us.

◀ A 2006 ad announcing our 'Perfekt' range of diamond jewellery featuring Bollywood actor Bhumik Chawla. It was a pioneering product in both the Indian and the Middle Eastern markets.

▲ An ad announcing the opening of our massive showroom in Chennai in 2008, featuring eye-catching visuals.

▲ Proudly receiving the 2008 Dubai Quality Appreciation Programme Award from none other than H.H. Sheikh Mohammed Bin Rashid Al Maktoum, vice-president and prime minister of UAE, and ruler of Dubai.

◀ The Alukka's clan on late Amma's remembrance day in 2008. Back row from left: I, Jacintha, Anto, Paul, Francis, Clara, Jos and Pauly. Front row from left: Philomina, Lucy, Rosily, Elsi, Mary, Kochuthresya and Reena.

◀ Receiving the 'Superbrand in the Middle East' award for the first time in 2010, a status we retained for eight years, even as we were debuting among the Superbrands in India.

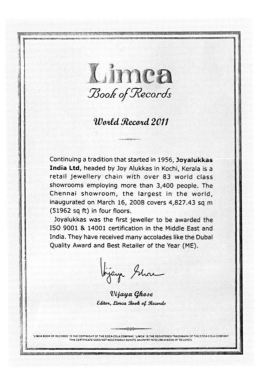

▲ A blood donation awareness campaign in association with Dubai Health Authority in 2012.

▲ The certificate from the Limca Book of Records in 2011 declaring Joyalukkas, T. Nagar, Chennai, as the largest gold jewellery showroom in the world—a record yet to be broken.

▶ We rebranded our fashion and silk retail business 'Wedding Centre' to 'Jolly Silks' in 2012. An ad featuring Bollywood actor Vidya Balan promoting the new identity of the brand.

◀ The staff at our flagship Dubai store receiving the 2018 'Best Service Performance Outlet Award' from Shaikha Ahmad Al Bishri, director of the Business Excellence department, Dubai Economy.

At the signing ceremony of AED 500 million dirhams term loan based on innovative POS security structure, held in Dubai. Growth capital to fund our expansion came from Standard Chartered, Mashreq and Emirates NBD. It was awarded the 'Best Regional Structured Trade Finance Solution' at the 2016 Asset Asian Awards (AAA) in Hong Kong.

With the all-star cast of celebrities who served as our brand ambassadors, in 2013. With actors Sudeep Sanjeev, R.K. Madhavan, Suresh Gopi and Allu Arjun.

The inauguration of our first store in Singapore, on Serangoon Road, Little India by our then brand mbassador, R.K. Madhavan, in April 2012.

▲ With my family during Elsa's graduation ceremony at Les Roches, Switzerland in 2019.

▲ The Joy Alukkas family: Jolly and I with our children, their spouses and our six grandchildren. Standing from left: Antony, Mary, Thomas, Elsa, Sonia and John. Sitting from left: Thea, Julia, Jos, Lionel Joy, Hazel and Michelle.

selected showrooms personally, because I can instinctively size up their potential.

I had carefully selected the city of Kottayam as the site for my first store. The district itself is flanked by the Western Ghats on the east and the Vembanad Lake and the paddy fields of Kuttanad on the west. Famous for its rubber plantations, it accounts for one-third of India's rubber production. It also has the highest number of expatriates in the Gulf, Europe and the USA. Both factors contribute to its prosperity. Thus, in terms of purchasing power, Kottayam was a great location for a jewellery store.

I knew that diamonds would increasingly feature in modern trends in South Indian bridal jewellery. Customers in Kerala were typically more concerned with the quality of the stones than their size. Kottayam, I felt, offered a ready market for quality diamonds. So, I took the risk of showcasing 600 carats of diamonds, whereas other jewellers were testing the market with a mere 50–100 carats. With our offerings in Kottayam, we introduced a wide variety of diamond jewellery to the market.

Our main requirement was a ready-to-move building where I could start the fit-out of the store interiors immediately. The Muthoot building on Kottayam's T.B. Road was exactly what we needed.

As for staffing, I personally screened 200 candidates and selected forty. For me, the first set of employees at my very first store in India will always be special. After their training, they set about contacting and inviting 50,000 households in Kottayam to patronize our store.

At 10.30 a.m. on 18 August 2002, Alukkas International formally debuted in India, welcoming the residents of

Kottayam to our lavish showroom with much fanfare. The managing director of the World Gold Council, Bryan Parker, did the honours, and I am pleased to say that my dear friend Jassim flew down for the event.

Meanwhile, after my family had settled into our villa in Dubai, Amma came to stay with us for a while. It was her fourth visit to Dubai. I would drive her around, show her our stores and take her on exploratory tours of the emirate. Jolly and Amma got along famously, in perfect sync with each other on matters of religion. Amma and the children, too, got along like a house on fire.

On 17 December 2002, a week before the much-anticipated Christmas eve, my beloved Amma, the iron lady of our house, left us. She had had a heart attack. I was in India when I heard the awful news. It saddened me profoundly, but the fact that Amma had spent her final days with us in Dubai was a blessing.

As always, I sought solace in my work. We had received an excellent response in Kottayam, and this encouraged me to launch stores in Angamaly, Thodupuzha, Thiruvalla and Kollam. While I was in India opening store after store, Jolly was taking care of John, who was eighteen at the time, Mary who was fifteen, and our youngest, Elsa, aged nine. I was working round the clock with no idea whether it was day or night, and living out of a suitcase. I would go from the office to the airport and vice versa. This naturally left me with very little time for my family. My daughters complained of my absence, and I missed them too. But I was consumed with work; the show had to go on.

Alukkas also stepped into fashion retail at this time. The idea originated one afternoon at a restaurant in Kochi. I had spent the morning holding meetings at my office, and had not had anything except two cups of black coffee. I found myself starving, and headed to the Abad Plaza hotel, which had a popular restaurant known for its excellent Kerala cuisine. The place was jam-packed and I was told that I would have to wait for half an hour to get a table.

Unwilling to wait that long, I asked a waiter to find me a seat. The only available chair was at a table already occupied by ten members of a family. I placed my order with the waiter and took my seat. In no time at all, my meal arrived and I polished it off in five minutes flat. Then, I turned my attention to the other people at the table, and as is my habit, opened a conversation. I asked them where they were from and what had brought them to Kochi.

The gentleman sitting next to me explained that they were in the city to shop for a wedding. 'I find the distances between outlets are too vast, be it for wedding wear, jewellery, footwear or other accessories. Going from one to the other is very cumbersome when you have close to a dozen family members accompanying you. I wish everything was under one roof,' he said.

It was a eureka moment. The idea of a Joyalukkas Wedding Centre, with jewellery, apparel and accessories under one roof, was born. The experience described by the gentleman at the restaurant was not an unusual one. In Kerala, shopping for a wedding is a collective exercise. A dozen or so members of a family would arrive from their town or village, spend a day or two purchasing jewellery and another day looking for sarees, footwear and accessories. If they could get all the items at the same location, they would save on time, energy and transportation costs.

We developed the 'ponnum podavayum orumich' (jewellery and textiles together) concept. We found an expert in textiles to source a wide collection of wedding wear for us. In 2003, we inaugurated our Wedding Centre at Angamaly, and it proved to be a grand success. Our second Wedding Centre opened at Thiruvalla, and the third at Kollam, both in 2004. The Wedding Centres were rebranded to 'Jolly Silks' in 2012.

I made it a special point to invite Jos to each and every inauguration. After all, he was the eldest in the family, with Amma now gone. In fact, all my brothers and sisters were invited and rarely failed to attend. At every inauguration, Jos extended his blessings. But he became more and more critical of me. I responded with a polite smile and held my peace. In our undeclared game of one-upmanship, my quick expansion must have been an irritant.

In 2004, matters came to a head when I invited him to the opening of my showroom in Coimbatore. It was my fifth store in India, and the largest at that point of time, covering 6,400 square feet. It was also my first foray outside Kerala.

Coimbatore was a challenging market, dominated by players with a legacy of fifty years or more. My co-worker P.D. Francis was assigned the task of cracking the market. He was stationed in the city for six months, during which he undertook a thorough study and did all the groundwork for the launch of our store.

In the course of our market survey, the head of our diamond division, Suresh V.N., observed that customers in Coimbatore were highly educated, on par with professional jewellers when it came to verifying the quality of stones. They would carry magnifying glasses to examine the diamonds before making a purchase. It was widely believed that stones of good quality brought good luck and prosperity to the wearer, whereas those of inferior quality had an adverse effect. So, customers literally left no stone unturned in assessing the diamonds.

The store proved a success. One of the reasons was that Alukkas came to be regarded as 'rashi ana kada' (fortune-bringing store). The belief originated with the sales of a traditional item of jewellery, the 'thali' (a gold pendant tied around the bride's neck by the groom as part of the wedding ritual). Demand for 'thalis' of various designs, depending on the caste or sub-caste of the wearer, escalated. We came up with more than a hundred designs, and in the process, became the city's go-to family jeweller. Along with traditional designs, we brought in more and more international offerings, while maintaining our superior quality standards.

For some reason, the Coimbatore showroom proved to be the last straw for Jos. When I went to his office to request him to light the 'nilavilakku' lamp (a traditional feature of inaugural ceremonies) at the opening, I was subjected to a rant. 'This is my office,' he snarled. 'Don't you ever come here again. I know why you're inviting me.'

Perhaps he was irritated because for every snarky remark he made, I opened another store.

The Coimbatore store was so successful that it gave me the confidence to enter unexplored markets outside Kerala. Subsequently, I made my first leap to the north with an outlet in Gurgaon (now Gurugram) in the National Capital Region. The following year, we opened an outlet in Delhi. More stores followed, including another first—in Andhra Pradesh (now Telangana), at Panjagutta in Hyderabad.

The Auction

Why did Jos seem constantly peeved with me? I do not have a clear answer to that question. Perhaps his resentment of me had deepened after the events of November 2002, at that fateful meeting of the five Alukkas brothers in Thrissur.

As we sat down at the Alukkas Hotel for the auction of the family properties, none of my brothers were aware that I had subtly manoeuvred them into the whole exercise.

Jos' obduracy on the Thiruvananthapuram showroom and our confrontation over the Mangalya Mela had eroded my faith in his sense of fair play. Resolving not to be short-changed again, I decided that we needed neutral parties to referee the negotiations on the disposal of the real estate assets. I homed in on three individuals with a strong background in finance, who were well-known to the Alukkas. I knew that Venugopal, Gopinath (who was Jos' financial advisor) and Pattabiraman, another auditor close to the family, would be acceptable to Jos.

I paid a visit to Pattabiraman at his house. While I was sitting with him, the idea of holding an auction struck me. So, I suggested it to him, and wrote out the conditions then and there. The bid amount was to be twenty-five lakh rupees, and 25 per cent of the total amount was to be paid within a month or two, with the balance remitted within the year.

Pattabiraman spoke to Jos and mooted the idea of an auction. Jos thought Pattabiraman had come up with the notion on his own, and agreed to it.

Jos was under the impression that he was the only one in the family who had the wherewithal to bid during the auction. As for me, while I did not have liquid cash, I was reasonably confident of being able to get funding from a bank. It was a gamble, but one I was willing to take. For me, the money was secondary. I was motivated by the intent and the will to challenge the status quo.

The seating arrangements at the auction were well thought-out. There were eight of us—five brothers and three financial advisers. Each sibling was separated by an auditor. No one was inclined to talk, and the expression on every face was solemn.

Other than me, everyone present expected the bidding to be a perfunctory exercise, with Jos making a clean sweep of all the properties. My other brothers were mere spectators, although they did have a stake in the auction. The higher the bid, the more money they would get as their share.

The first item to come up was the hotel that had a bar licence, along with the hospital. I took that. In the second round of bidding, another two properties came up and I acquired them as well.

At one stage, Jos lost his temper and ranted at Venugopal. After he had calmed down and regained his composure, he apologized. But the drama was just beginning.

In the final round, the properties under auction were the Puzhakkal land, the Alukkas Gardens and a three-acre hill. At this point, Jos instructed me not to bid because he wanted those properties for himself.

Of all the assets, the Puzhakkal land, measuring around fifty-five acres, was a special bone of contention. Jos had managed to stall its sale for years, because he had his eye on it.

We could never convince a buyer to pick up the land because Jos would immediately demand an absurdly exorbitant price for it.

Neither of us were willing to let go of the land, and we kept outbidding each other. Venugopal, as a conscientious financial consultant, was horrified as I was going beyond my budget. Since he could not protest out aloud, he repeatedly kicked my leg, indicating that I should stop bidding forthwith. I ignored him.

By now, Jos was in a fine fury and he threw a tantrum. 'If you bid for this last property, Joy, I will quit the auction,' he thundered.

At that juncture, everyone intervened and asked me to desist. I had made my point and could afford to be generous. In any case, the land did not really mean much to me. My intention had been to speed up the process and be done with it. I stopped bidding and allowed Jos to pick up the land.

The auction ended on this sour note. In 2005, Jos sold the land for a huge profit. Fifteen years down the line, it has become a thriving development with excellent infrastructure, known as 'Sobha City'.

The other siblings did not do too badly either. Although they had not bid for any of the properties, they did get their share in cash, considerably more than they would have without the auction. As for me, I did not ask for any property either before or after the partition. I was content with whatever I had bought.

I walked away from the auction, a free man. Now I could run my business any way I pleased. I could be adventurous and make my own mistakes.

One of my first independent decisions was to put up the hotel for sale, as I did not want the Alukkas name to be associated with a bar!

The House of Alukkas

I have often wondered where the house of Alukkas might be if we had not partitioned the business. Would we have been far more significant together than we are individually? Perhaps, but on the other hand, I may not have done as well as I have. On balance, I think it was for the best. While I know of several joint family businesses in India that are doing well, that may be because all the shareholders are in perfect accord, operating like a single entity.

The five Alukkas brothers, on the other hand, had different viewpoints on business. We would have been forced to compromise at every step to keep the peace, and that would have been a serious handicap in the growth of the business. Instead of striving for excellence, we may have settled for mediocrity.

As it happened, we wound up in competition with each other, which need not have been the case. I know of a family in Kerala in which all the siblings are in the jewellery business, but operate independently and under the same brand name. They have a mutual understanding; if one brother operates in one city, then the other will not open a store in the same vicinity and become a competitor.

The Alukkas had no such agreement, but none of my brothers expected me to open a store in their areas of operation. At the outset, I was certainly careful not to set up

stores in cities where my brothers already had their showrooms.
I deliberately avoided north Kerala, where Francis operated.
I also gave Thrissur and Thiruvananthapuram a wide berth to
avoid stepping on Jos and Anto's toes. Likewise, I stayed away
from Ernakulam, where Paul was stationed. All of these cities
were excellent markets in terms of jewellery consumption, but
I preferred to go south, so as not to proffer direct competition
to my brothers.

All that changed when Jos decided to challenge me on my
own turf, after having elicited my support for his own business.
Before the Mangalya Mela, he had approached me, saying that
he wanted to set up a wholesale business in Dubai. He gave
me to understand that the objective was to procure designer
jewellery from Dubai for his showrooms in India. I happily
agreed to introduce him to my sponsor, Jassim Al Hasawi.

Jos' son came to Dubai to look after the operation. Later,
they told me that they wanted to open a retail store—just
one—to break even on their expenses in the wholesale unit.
I agreed, and they inaugurated a showroom dubbed the
'House of Alukkas' in the Gold Centre building. Jassim chose
to relinquish his role as Jos' sponsor when my brother moved
into retail.

Contrary to my expectations, Jos decided to expand,
without keeping me in the loop. They followed it up with a
second outlet in the Karama area, and then a store in Sharjah.
The fact that they used the name House of Alukkas and we
operated under 'Alukkas Jewellery' created considerable
confusion in brand recall.

I decided to confront Jos. 'I didn't come to your place for
competition, and that was the understanding when we went

through with the partition,' I said. In a flash of anger, Jos said, 'There is no such rule, you can open wherever you want, even in Thrissur. I have no objection.' I was free to do so, but I don't think he seriously thought I would.

Gradually, our interactions with each other became like a game of chess, with both parties making tactical moves and counter-moves.

As it turned out, the House of Alukkas didn't survive in the Dubai market; they closed all their stores and by 2006, had left the UAE. Jos and his sons, as business owners, had failed to understand that all markets have different dynamics. Each one needs a tailor-made approach, because there is no such thing as 'one size fits all'.

Two decades after Alukkas was partitioned, I can categorically say that I have found sole leadership an excellent way to operate. Like a ship, a company needs one captain and a clear chain of command. I have maintained that order and clarity in my enterprises. Too many leaders pulling in different directions impedes progress.

So, did the partition erode my strength or spirit? Not at all. It rekindled my ambitions, and gave me a new vision and a fresh purpose. It brought clarity to my thoughts, and delineated the path ahead. I promised myself that I would change the face of the industry.

Meanwhile, the face of Dubai itself was changing. On 4 January 2006, H.H. Sheikh Mohammed bin Rashid Al Maktoum, crown prince of Dubai and minister of defence of the UAE, was crowned ruler of Dubai after the demise of his brother, H.H. Sheikh Maktoum bin Rashid. Under Sheikh Mohammed's leadership, Dubai emerged as a global city with megaprojects like the Burj Khalifa, the Dubai Marina, the Dubai Metro, the Dubai Mall and the Palm Islands. There was a new energy, an air of vibrancy and a sense of great things to come. It was impossible not to feel optimistic about the future—I certainly did.

I still remember a journalist asking me during a media interaction in Dubai, back in 2004, about my vision for the future. 'A hundred stores in ten countries with a one-billion-dollar turnover by 2010,' I replied. Thereafter, I woke up every morning with a recollection of that resolve.

8

The World's No. 1
22-Karat Jeweller

'Joy, are you aware that you're the world's top jeweller?' asked my friend Ravi Prasad. I thought he was pulling my leg, so I just smiled and murmured, 'Do you really think so?' He frowned, and I realized he wasn't joking. As an advertising director, Ravi saw the world through the lens of branding, sales, product offering and customer perception. Clearly, his fertile brain had come up with an idea.

Sure enough, he launched into his pitch, which was based on three points. First, we had sixteen outlets, more than any other single entity in the UAE. Second, unlike the traditional jewellers in the Gulf and the West, who sold only 18-karat gold, we dealt exclusively in 22-karat products. Third, we had the widest, most eclectic range of designs. In effect, that made us the No. 1 22-karat jeweller!

I had met Ravi in 1993. He was a marketing man, who had held senior positions in several companies in India before joining the advertising agency Madco Gulf, which had the World Gold Council as their exclusive client. I had just two stores at the time, but even then, I was open to the idea of experimenting with marketing and brand building, and was willing to put money into it, although finances were extremely tight. The two of us got along very well.

In 2000, Ravi became the account director of Madco Gulf, which I subsequently retained. Having ideas on brand promotion and positioning is one thing, but translating them into full-fledged campaigns is another. I had realized that a good advertising agency, which knew just what I wanted and executed it professionally, was a sine qua non. Ravi understood my vision. Not just that, he added to and embellished the ideas I shared with him. So, when he came up with the notion of positioning Alukkas as the 'No. 1 22-karat jeweller', I listened to him seriously.

He was right about the expansion part. In 2000 alone, five new showrooms had materialized, including one at the Gold Land building and two in Abu Dhabi. We made inroads into Bahrain with a store in Manama. Another showroom was opened at Dubai's Al Qusais shopping mall, owned by the Lulu Group, which had been founded by a fellow denizen of Thrissur, Yusuff Ali M.A. We were also slated to reopen our newly renovated store at the Gold Centre, Dubai Gold Souk.

Ravi's logic was that if we didn't promote ourselves as an industry leader, who would? As he pointed out, customers were invariably attracted to the biggest brand in the business, and took pride in gifting or wearing items with the label.

Were we actually No. 1 at that point? That was a matter of perspective—and Ravi's ingenuity. Certainly, my retail chain was the exception in an era of standalone jewellers, and as I catered to Indian tastes, we sold only 22-karat gold. I couldn't help but agree that there was ample justification for the claim. I gave him the go-ahead.

The advertisement, when it came out, was a masterpiece of subtlety and flair. It depicted a shining vertical stack of gold bangles, a veritable tower or pillar of gold that represented the numeral '1'.

'Alukkas: The No. 1 in 22-Karat Jewellery', read the text. It wasn't just another advertisement; it conveyed, through actual numbers, where we stood at the time. Alukkas was the top jeweller in the 22-karat space in terms of our store network, range of designs and customer service. The phrases '5,00,000 satisfied customers', '50,000 designs', '20,000 square feet of showroom space' and '16 exclusive showrooms' referred to all three elements.

A stunningly bold move, it captured the imagination of customers across the Gulf, and became a talking point in the industry. It gave us an image greater than our market presence. The first in a series of highly successful campaigns, which helped the brand stay several steps ahead of the competition, it was a milestone event in our journey. That golden tower was to become Alukkas' signature.

We deployed it again for our iconic Rolls Royce campaign, mentioned in the prologue. I walked into Ravi's office and said, 'Can we do a campaign around "buy jewellery from Alukkas and win a Rolls Royce"?'. Ravi half-rose from his chair; his expression one of shock. Gradually, the idea sunk in and we began to discuss it. He was sure it would work; in a city full of Toyota Corollas, Nissan Sunnys and BMW 3 Series, owning a Rolls Royce was in the realm of fantasy. It had an unmatched 'wow' factor.

We decided to dovetail the Rolls Royce promotion with our earlier 'No. 1 22-Karat Jeweller' campaign. The advertisements publicizing the offer featured the tower of gold, capped with the 'Spirit of Ecstasy' hood ornament. It was a bold attempt to conjoin Rolls Royce and Alukkas: the legendary No. 1 car, and the leading gold retailer. So, apart from triggering immediate purchases, the campaign contributed significantly to the brand-building process. As mentioned earlier, it was the first time that a jeweller had offered an ultra-luxury car in a raffle draw, and it shook up not only the entire industry but all of Dubai. As my friend Ashraf, regional sales head of Al Habtoor Motors (the Rolls Royce dealers), recalls: 'Giving away a Rolls Royce car in a raffle was a novel idea. Dubai Duty Free could do it, but individual business owners never thought of it.'

We advertised widely in the print and broadcast media, creating such a sensation that people who had no interest in cars or jewellery were talking about it. Once, when I was passing through the Dubai airport immigration, the officer checking my passport and visa saw my name and that of the company. He looked up at me and asked, 'Are you the one who is doing the Rolls Royce campaign?'

Some people thought it was a gimmick, others speculated that it was a used car. At the time, only the royal family rode around in Rolls Royces! In fact, the Silver Seraph was only in production for four years, with just 1,570 units produced.

Now, of course, many expat Indians in Dubai have opted for the luxury car.

The promotion was conducted from 17 June to 13 October 2000, all across the Gulf, so apart from the Dubai authorities, we needed approvals from Qatar, Oman and Bahrain. Justin Sunny, who was the manager of our Bahrain store at the time, was able to get a quick go-ahead from the Bahrain Promotion Board, only to be called back the very next day and told that permission had been withdrawn. This was a significant setback, because an assent from Bahrain would have enabled us to get swift and simultaneous approvals from the other Gulf Cooperation Council (GCC) countries.

Our Rolls Royce campaign was all set for a full roll-out, with all the artwork, media buys, store merchandising and printed raffle tickets in place. Now, everything had to be put on hold.

The Bahrain Promotion Board members were apprehensive that since the Rolls Royce was not physically present in their country, running newspaper ads publicizing the promotion might be deemed inappropriate. We approached them with a compromise; we would advertise only through flyers, in-store promotions and merchandising. Even so, bringing them around was tough. But we finally got permission, and after that, obtaining approvals from Oman, Qatar and the UAE was easy.

The promotion went forward, and we saw an uptick in sales, with Emiratis who had no desire to buy jewellery picking up coupons, just so that they could have a chance to win the iconic car.

The raffle draw was transparent, conducted by the local authorities of Dubai. As it happened, the winner was

Bahrain-based, an Indian expat from Kerala. I was to hand over a giant thermocol key to him onstage, for the benefit of the photographers. But the lucky winner refused to take the key, assuming that if he accepted it, he would not get the prize, so the photo session was cancelled. However, he agreed to take delivery of the car. Later, we learnt that he had sold it (at a discounted price). The reasoning behind the campaign was sound. Any new entrant to the Gulf comes with a three-point agenda: finding a job, obtaining a driving licence and owning a car! From the very beginning, I was a great votary of car promotions because of their mass appeal. At first, the other jewellers objected. My response was to buy another twelve Mitsubishi cars from my friend Ashraf and put them up in a raffle. Later, my detractors realized that it was an effective tool for boosting sales, and followed suit. Every three months, there would be a car promotion, and if someone offered two cars, I would offer ten.

Coining a Campaign

During my initial phase of expansion and brand-building, I maintained a close working relationship with the World Gold Council. It was in both our interests to boost the consumption of gold. I collaborated with them for the launch of one of our most unique products: a medallion which we dubbed the 'One World Coin', to commemorate the 'One World, One Family, One Festival' theme of DSF 2001.

It was a fourteen-gram coin in 24-karat gold, and it was intended to capture the cosmopolitan spirit of Dubai. I conceived it as a product that had three virtues: beauty, value and symbolism. Thus, it had a utilitarian element, because of the intrinsic value of the gold, as well as an aesthetic appeal. It also had emotional content, as it represented the essence of our common home. Dubai is known for its liberalism and pluralism, values that are cherished in the modern world. It is a living embodiment of unity in diversity, with communities, ethnicities, religions and classes coexisting and thriving together. So, the message had to be one of 'global harmony'.

The theme was exemplified in the design of the coin: a circle of people, ringed around the globe, with the message 'Together in Harmony' in English and Arabic. The other side simply had the globe, with the words 'One World Coin' in both languages. We presented the sample to the Dubai Gold and Jewellery Group, and they liked both the product and the proposed campaign. They asked me to go ahead with it.

The coin was manufactured by PAMP, one of the world's largest and most reputed gold refineries, located in Switzerland. Ravi had worked with PAMP, and he used that relationship to ensure a product of the very highest quality. We ordered five thousand coins, weighing seventy kilograms in total. The finishing was excellent, and each coin was priced at 500 dirhams.

My innovation in terms of marketing was to make the coin available to all, and not keep it exclusive to Alukkas. Yes, it was a departure from the traditional approach, but I felt that keeping it to ourselves would go against the very spirit of the message we were trying to convey.

Besides, the World Gold Council was funding half the cost of promotions and advertising, and they were keen on the widest possible distribution. In their view, a high-value, fast-moving product was in the best interest of their members, as it meant more sales of gold. So, we decided that any retail outlet in the Gulf could buy and distribute the coins.

Before we could sell a single piece in Dubai, we ran into a snag. I hadn't counted on the negative attitude of our competition. Someone pointed out that the word 'coin' was engraved on the product, whereas only the State has the right to mint coins.

Technically, it was a violation of sovereignty, which would ordinarily have gone unnoticed, as a variety of agencies, including jewellers, sell gold coins and biscuits. But once the complaint had been made, we had to take cognizance of it.

I mulled over the problem of offloading five thousand gold coins. Melting them down was definitely not an option. I talked it over with Renjith and P.D. Jose. We came up with the idea of sending the coins to our showrooms in Bahrain, Qatar and Oman, as we did not anticipate any issues there.

My team rose to the occasion magnificently. They endeavoured to sell three to four coins to each customer, and for the most part, they succeeded. From the first day onwards, we met our daily sales target. We also dovetailed the One World Coin with a car promotion. Customers who purchased the fourteen-gram coin could participate in a raffle draw to win an S-class Mercedes-Benz.

Meanwhile, our expansion spree in the Gulf continued. In May 2001, our very first showroom in the emirate of Ras Al-Khaimah opened its doors. A new store in Sharjah, our second in Muscat and one in Bur Dubai followed. Both in terms of footprint and visibility, Alukkas was making its presence felt, with aggressive promotional campaigns that generated a lot of buzz around the brand. But more than anything else, what was important to me was our reputation for reliability and impeccable quality standards.

Credibility, Quality, Purity

Purity of gold is of prime importance in the jewellery trade, and here's why. As any customer knows, gold is the most ductile and malleable of metals; it can be drawn into a very fine wire or flattened into a very thin sheet. On the other hand, 24-karat gold of 99.9 per cent purity is far too soft for jewellery, as it cannot withstand everyday wear.

To strengthen gold, silver and copper are added to create an alloy of 91.6 per cent purity, that is, 22-karat gold. This age-old practice, unfortunately, made it hard to standardize gold jewellery. As a result, patrons had to buy gold ornaments on faith, trusting in their jeweller. Quite often, they were unaware that the gold they purchased was of 90–91 per cent purity, that is, 21-karat rather than 22-karat.

While purity standards were inconsistent in India, they were rigorously enforced in the Gulf countries; so much so that, as mentioned earlier, 'Dubai gold' became the quality norm for the precious metal from the 1990s onwards. This factor, more than any other, contributed to the UAE's dominance of the global gold trade.

Quality assurance is essential to win the customer's trust and loyalty, and this in turn is an imperative in our business. Integrity in our dealings with our patrons has always been an article of faith for me. Never, ever must we break faith with the customer by compromising on the quality of our products. They must enter our stores in the absolute knowledge that the purity of the gold they purchase from us is beyond doubt.

From the very start of my business in the UAE, I was faced with the challenge of ensuring the purity of the gold jewellery I imported from India. Given the superiority of—and demand for—traditional Indian designs, I leveraged the synergy of our stores in India and the UAE and imported directly from our manufacturers in Kerala. In fact, I had an edge over our competitors in terms of design.

Even before regulations were put in place, Alukkas adhered strictly to the purity requirements in India and the Gulf. As a result, we gained credibility in the market. On the flip side, unscrupulous players who flouted purity standards were able to undercut prices and this adversely affected our bottom line in India.

Our response was to educate the consumer. From 1996, Alukkas began advertising in Kerala's leading dailies, explaining the concept of 22-karat gold and 91.6 per cent purity. The blowback from jewellery retail associations and other major retailers in Kerala was massive. They took out ads with the counter-claim that '916 gold' was a way of cheating the customer by charging inflated prices, and also picketed our stores in Thrissur and Kozhikode. Alukkas stood alone on its side of the fence, with all the other jewellers on the other side.

We not only stuck to our guns, but doubled down on our ad campaign. So did our opposition, with the result that the ad, revenues of the Thrissur edition of all the leading newspapers spiked! Gradually, the campaign took effect and customers began demanding 91.6 per cent purity from their jewellers.

When my brother, Anto, opened his new store in the year 1998 in Kunnamkulam, Kerala, he announced that it would sell ornaments of '916 purity' only. This was, perhaps, the first store in India to showcase gold of strictly this purity. Our competitors were forced to set up counters for '916 jewellery' in all their stores.

In other parts of India, however, jewellers continued to sell ornaments of diluted purity touted as 22-karat. It was only in 2021 that the government of India stepped in and made hallmarking mandatory. Alukkas can proudly say that we were the pioneers of 916 gold in India. Today, jewellers cannot retail 22-karat ornaments without the Bureau of Indian Standards (BIS) Hallmark Unique Identification (HUID) number on the jewellery.

This brings us to the question of assaying gold. The old method of using touchstones was obviously arbitrary by contemporary standards. One reason why a sure-fire assay method is needed lies in the very nature of the gold trade. Recycling of old jewellery is the norm, and constitutes one-third of all sales. Customers barter old pieces for new designs, and pay only the making/design charges. The old jewellery is melted down and used for manufacturing new pieces.

We found that the jewellery brought in by customers from India contained a very high percentage of impurities. If we subjected the pieces to fire or acid assay—which in any case was only possible in a gold refinery—they would be mutilated. An easier and non-destructive method of gauging purity was needed.

Enter the X-Ray Fluorescence Spectrometer. The technology had been patented in Japan, and the machine was aimed at the Middle East and India markets. The DGJG invited all the UAE jewellers to a demonstration. The spectrometer identifies elements and their quantity in any object. With the aid of computer software, it accurately measured gold purity in less than five minutes, without so much as a scratch on the jewellery.

The machine was expensive, at 1,10,000 dirhams, but so convinced was I of its efficacy, and indeed its necessity, that I instructed my team to place an order at once. We rolled it out at all our showrooms and it came to be known among customers and trade insiders as the purity analyser. In no time at all, every major jeweller in the Gulf followed suit. Anto was the first to adopt it in Kerala. He had to face considerable opposition initially, mainly from jewellers' associations. Today, the purity analyser is a prerequisite for any jewellery showroom.

My point is that transparency and trust is the very soul of the gold business. I have always fought for what I believe in, and that made us front-runners in the adoption and promotion of purity standards.

Wooing the Customer

In jewellery retail, customer appreciation gifts are the norm. Freebies tend to put a smile on the customer's face and increase their level of satisfaction. Over the years, Alukkas gave away sarees, 'mundum neriyathum' (women's traditional mundu set), perfumes, boxes of sweets, airline tickets and even mobile phone connections.

But when all your competitors follow the same practice, it doesn't necessarily ensure brand loyalty or customer retention. So, I hit upon an innovative method of wooing customers and making them feel special. The jewellery industry was moving away from traditional gifting ideas and innovation was the need of the hour.

As a frequent flyer of Emirates, I had enrolled in its class-apart loyalty programme. I wanted to grow Alukkas' customer base along the same lines, by offering value to its customers around the world, so that they could earn and enjoy rewards conveniently.

Towards the end of 2004, we launched the first-ever loyalty programme in the jewellery industry: the Alukkas Golden Reward card for 'privileged' patrons. In a major coup, we got the reigning superstar of Bollywood, Shah Rukh Khan, a.k.a. 'King' Khan, to come on board the loyalty programme as its first member.

'SRK' and his troupe were on the 'Temptation 2004' tour, entertaining fans in various countries. They had held shows in Atlanta, New York and London before arriving in the UAE. As the title sponsor of the Dubai show—the first of its kind in the city, dubbed 'Alukkas Temptation'—I used my leverage to get SRK to endorse our loyalty programme.

A press conference was scheduled as a curtain raiser to the show. A day earlier, I went to meet SRK at the hotel where he was staying. The corridor was lined with female fans who had queued up in the hope of catching a glimpse of their idol. I was escorted to his suite, where he greeted me with his famously infectious smile. He addressed me as 'Joy sahib', and put me at my ease. Lighting a cigarette, he spoke to me as if we were old friends who had met after a long hiatus. As he took puff after puff, I couldn't resist advising him to give up smoking. He flashed a smile at me in response, but didn't say anything. All in all, I found him a vibrant, charming personality.

One Woman, 100,000 Expressions

By 2000, it had become obvious to me that consumer tastes were changing, so we had to change as well. Alongside the traditionally Indian, the demand for more modern and lightweight designs was growing, as was the appetite for gemstone jewellery. There were two elements to the transition. First, I wanted to impart an international look and calibre to our brand. Second, I had conceptualized 'alukkas' (later Joyalukkas) as a jewellery 'hub', as opposed to a jewellery 'store'.

This meant going beyond our identity as the 'No. 1' among 22-karat gold jewellers, both in terms of product offerings and reach. To that end, we needed to expand our range, especially that of gemstone-studded or precious jewellery. I decided that we would showcase eclectic collections in different precious metals (gold, silver and platinum) to suit all preferences, budgets and occasions. Thereby, we would broaden our customer base across demographics, income segments and geographies.

While I had conceived 'alukkas' as the umbrella brand for our retail business, I wanted to create sub-brands distinct from the product lines already on offer. Designer jewellery would command bigger margins, as customers are willing to spend more on exclusive products. The appeal of haute couture labels lies in their cachet and glamour, intangibles that are of value to the aspirational consumer and create an emotional connect with the brand. I wanted a similar aura around 'alukkas'.

A powerful brand cannot be built overnight. It demands continual investment in product innovation, branding and marketing. So, we got down to the business of creating several sub-brands, each offering a distinct collection of jewellery. A 'collection' refers to ornaments—bangles, rings, nose pins, necklaces, etc.—that are tied together by a single theme.

Meanwhile, the World Gold Council, confronted by the shift away from yellow gold and heavy, chunky gold jewellery, was looking to counter the trend. The way forward, it decided, was to support a leading jewellery retailer in a campaign that would popularize gold while catering to consumer preferences.

Our ad agency at the time was Amber Communications. Sudhir Nair, the agency's CEO, conceived of a campaign centred around the notion of 'One Woman, 100,000 Expressions'. The WGC liked the concept and agreed to fund half the cost of the campaign. Initially, the idea was to portray a teenager as young as fourteen transitioning to adulthood and marriage, while showcasing age-appropriate jewellery at each stage of her journey. Later, it morphed into a focus on her 'expressions', referring to the synergy between her moods and her jewellery, through different settings and stages of life.

It was our first international TV campaign, and signalled a shift in our design philosophy. Henceforth, we would offer the traditional, the modern, and a fusion of both, with '1,00,000' designs to choose from. The customer would be spoiled for choice, with ornaments to fit every mood.

The tagline positioned jewellery as a mode of self-expression. A woman's choice of ornaments reflects her unique personality and her frame of mind. Whatever attitude she chooses to channel—sassy, dramatic, understated, thoughtful—we, as her jeweller, enable the desired 'look'. The implication was that we don't just provide a piece of jewellery, but exemplify her state of mind.

The word 'expressions' carried another layer of meaning, drawing on the Indian concepts of 'rasa' or emotions, and 'shringar' or decoration. It referred to the many expressions that flit across a woman's face as she selects and embellishes herself with jewellery.

Sudhir advised us to deploy the 'star power' of a youthful Bollywood celebrity to enhance our appeal to the younger demographic—women who knew their minds and were financially empowered. The 'face' of our campaign had to represent the generation in transition, with traditional roots and a modern outlook. Our first choice was actor Kareena Kapoor, fresh from her breakthrough role in *Chameli*. She was feisty, yet earthy, and conveyed an enormous zest for life. We felt she would be the best fit for a campaign targeted at young women.

Shortly afterwards, I left for Mumbai to sign a contract with Kareena Kapoor, but it didn't materialize. The deal was cancelled at the very last minute. Unfazed by this setback, I asked my team to look for another 'face' for our campaign. They homed in on actor–model Chitrangada Singh. The winsome Chitrangada had a cosmopolitan appeal, and could elegantly carry off ethnic and western styles of apparel and jewellery.

We signed her up, and the shooting of the ad film commenced in Ooty, the idyllic hill-station in Tamil Nadu. It was directed by Rajeev Menon, an acclaimed filmmaker. Composer Ram Sampath wrote the music, and artiste

Sowmya Raoh rendered the theme song (it was later dubbed in Malayalam, and sung by eminent playback singer Sujatha Mohan).

For Rajeev, it was a maiden effort in the jewellery segment. He observed: 'It was very challenging to capture the smaller pieces of daily-wear jewellery in natural light. So, we used variations of hard and soft lights. Run-of-the-mill jewellery ads present the ideal bride embellished with jewellery; we wanted to popularize daily-wear jewellery on the girl next door. To show her enjoying normal activities without being self-conscious and carrying off her ornaments with ease in all settings and at all moments and events.'

The shooting was wrapped up in two weeks. We saw the rough cuts and they looked amazing. Anklets, bangles, waist chains, earrings, rings and necklaces: Chitrangada showcased them all with casual flair. The One Woman, 1,00,000 Expressions campaign grabbed eyeballs and ensured that 'alukkas' stood out from the other jewellers.

In a way, my learnings from nearly two decades of doing business in the Gulf set the stage for my next big leap—transitioning from Alukkas. There were many Alukkas by this time, but just one named Joy.

9

Putting the 'Joy' in Alukkas

꧁꧂

One of my great pleasures is driving, especially on the velvety-smooth roads of Dubai. When I am at the wheel and alone, I don't play music, preferring instead to look at the surrounding cityscape. I take note of new developments in road infrastructure and the evolution of the skyline, but what invariably draws my attention is advertising. Hoardings, billboards and signages are an endless source of fascination and occasionally, of ideas.

One evening in 2004, I was driving home from my office at the Deira Gold Land building to our villa in Al Mankhool, to which we had shifted in 2001. I stopped at a traffic signal just before the Al Shindagha tunnel (which runs under the Dubai Creek and connects the business districts of Deira and Bur Dubai). My eye caught a billboard of the legend Majid Al Futtaim Group.

Just then, the signal turned green and I was obliged to drive ahead and cross the tunnel. I reached Bur Dubai, took a U-turn and drove straight back. Once again, I approached the billboard and this time, I read it thoroughly. The idea that had begun to germinate with my first glimpse of the lettering was now full-blown. The additional four kilometres that the billboard had added to my journey had been worth it.

How did that billboard inspire me? The story that it told was well-known: the Al Futtaim group, with businesses across retail, services and manufacturing, had split in 2000. Majid had retained the family title in his company name, while adding his own.

The message for me, quite simply, was that I could keep my father's legacy alive, even while creating my own. I could cut the umbilical cord and yet, retain the goodwill, credibility and sterling reputation of the brand he had established.

So, I decided to add 'Joy' to 'Alukkas'. It was time to craft a new identity for myself and my business. For several years, ever since the partition of the family business in 2001 and the subsequent launch of my ventures in India, I had been looking for a way to differentiate my enterprises. Each of us was on his own and operating independently, but we were still connected through our brand name, 'Alukkas'.

The Need for a Rebrand

Jewellery at the time was regarded as a generic commodity, purchasable from any outlet. There was no premium brand positioning to evoke an emotional connect to the product. I saw this gap as an opportunity to build my brand. I wanted my showrooms to stand out. After all, the services and ambience we offered our customers were very different from that of other stores. Our promotional efforts and advertisements were far more eye-catching, and we went to great lengths to ensure an unparalleled customer experience. Our product range was different, as was our management style.

So, I changed the font size in the logo and added the word 'International' when I launched my business in India. It didn't serve the purpose. The modification was too slight to make an impression. As my footprint in India expanded, I was more and more convinced of the need for a unique identity. Customers thought that all the Alukkas stores were part of the same family enterprise. This caused confusion and created awkward situations. Given the lack of synergy between the businesses run by the Alukkas brothers, I was keen that my name and logo should convey that we were a separate entity.

As an inveterate problem-solver, I kept looking for a way to establish my exclusivity. Establishing a separate identity was not an easy decision, as I was and will always be proud of the brand that my father had created and I had perpetuated. It was a testimony to the passion and perseverance that characterized us both.

Sentimental reasons apart, it takes years to establish a brand, and giving it up was bound to affect my business adversely. Legacy and trust are crucial in the jewellery business. On the other hand, if I didn't create a brand-new identity, the USP of my business would get diluted in the long run.

We had tried to reposition ourselves in 2003, with the same name but a new logo spelling 'alukkas' in lower case instead of capital letters, and switching to a sans serif font. The change was small, but I felt that it served to give us a more modern touch while differentiating us from the other Alukkas stores.

Full-page advertisements were splashed across the major English dailies in the Gulf—and all the regional newspapers in South India. The imagery of 'Alukkas' transitioning through a horizontal series of gold bangles to the new brand 'alukkas' was creative, simple and yet compelling, clearly messaging that we were a different entity. But it did not have the desired effect. Jos taunted me, commenting, 'You are sloping from the big Alukkas to a small alukkas.'

I wanted to create a brand of my own. The challenge was to do so without losing the legacy factor. The brand had to be recognizable, yet unique. When I spotted the Majid Al Futtaim Group billboard, it occurred to me that most prominent jewellery houses are named after the founder or the family: such as Tiffany's, Cartier, Van Cleef & Arpels, Chopard and Buccellati.

So, sitting behind the wheel of my car in Dubai, I called Ravi Prasad. 'I want to rename alukkas,' I said without preamble. 'I want to change it to Joyalukkas.'

The next few months were incredibly hectic but exciting, as we ideated strategies to change our identity from 'alukkas' to the global brand 'Joyalukkas'. In so doing, I would be merging the two primary brand equities of 'alukkas': first, our legacy of trust and credibility and second, our status as the world's leading retailer of 22-karat gold jewellery. Rebranding occurred in parallel with repositioning. That process was already underway.

We committed huge resources to the marketing campaign and also applied for changing the names on all our licences, in the Gulf and in India. In January 2005, we decided to advertise our new identity. To pique interest and create suspense, we announced on the front pages of all the leading newspapers that 'alukkas' was changing its brand name.

The very next day, we ran our inaugural ad, unveiling our new catchphrase: 'Joyalukkas, the World's Favourite Jeweller'. It was eye-catching, with a visual of a gold locket open to reveal 'alukkas' on one side and 'Joyalukkas' on the other, and supported by the text 'heralding the birth of a new era'. It recalled the brand's heritage and its gradual transition in terms of nomenclature, as well as its standing as the leading jewellery retailer in the world. We played on the word 'joy' to ensure maximum recall.

Our previous signature slogan, 'The World's No. 1 22-Karat Jeweller', was no longer adequate, or even relevant to the positioning we had in mind. So, Sudhir had come up with the new tagline, which was more in keeping with an international brand: 'The World's Favourite Jeweller'.

Mass adjustment to the new name took a while. By force of habit, 'alukkas' was always on the tip of everyone's tongue, be it our suppliers, business associates or employees. It took them quite a while to get accustomed to it! A widespread misconception was that it was Joy Alukkas, two words rather than one. 'It's one word, Joyalukkas, the brand name,' I kept having to correct people.

Meanwhile, my team focused on changing our signages, hoardings, packaging bills, letterheads, business cards and so on, to reflect our new identity. Amending official documentation, like trade licences and visas, took an inordinate amount of time. It tested my patience, but there was little I could do to expedite the process. Eventually, every last item was in place, and Joyalukkas' journey began in earnest.

Incidentally, rebranding had never figured during the long-drawn out process of partition. News of this latest innovation soon reached my brothers. They were dumbfounded. 'Why did you change the name, Alukkas? It is the family brand!' they exclaimed. It confirmed their view that I was a maverick.

But the shock wore off after a while, and they saw just how fruitful the repositioning had been.

It is said that imitation is the highest form of flattery. They began to copy what I had done. Within a matter of a few years, my brothers changed their brand names one by one. I was amused. So much for my alleged lack of business sense. The fact was that they were seeking to reproduce a painting, without understanding the brushstrokes that went into creating it.

Wherever I opened a store, my brothers would follow. Customers noted that there was a difference in the names and would ask if the showrooms belonged to the same entity. Pat would come the reply: 'Yes, we are one company.' I wondered whether my silence endorsed the misconception that we were the same company.

Going Global

Post-rebranding, I was ready not only to go global, but to extend my business to money exchange (remittance of money and exchange of foreign currency). By the end of 2005, the influx of expats had bolstered the population of the UAE to over five million. I wanted to leverage our brand name and the trust it commanded among our clients to serve their money exchange needs. We began by acquiring one such exchange in Dubai, and subsequently penetrated other countries in the Gulf. Given the low-profit, high-volume nature of the business, it took us almost six years to break even.

On the jewellery front, having studied market trends, I surmised that there was a great demand globally for Indian ornaments. The burgeoning Indian diaspora in North America, Europe, Southeast Asia and Australia was a significant but underserved market. An estimated 13.2 million NRIs and PIOs lived overseas in 2010 (the current figure is eighteen million). Outside of the Middle East, the largest population of overseas Indians were in the USA, UK, Malaysia and Canada. We already had a big presence in the Middle East and India; now, the rest of the world beckoned.

My first move towards the internationalization of the brand was to register the intellectual property rights for 'Joyalukkas' in all my target markets. Simultaneously, I began looking for funding, as global expansion naturally called for a massive level of investment.

From 2006, Joyalukkas went truly international, with a showroom on Green Street, London. The location was carefully chosen—in the heart of a shopping area specializing in South Asian goods, including food, jewellery and fabrics. We followed it up with a showroom in Singapore. Even as we took baby steps in other markets, our growth trajectory in the Gulf and India kept rising.

The core elements of our strategy were: expansion of our footprint, innovative uber-luxury products, high-profile co-branding partnerships, use of star power, high-voltage promotional campaigns and top-notch quality standards.

Celebrities lent glamour to our brand, prominent among them the superstar of the Tamil film industry,

Ranganathan Madhavan, known simply as Madhavan, who had successfully crossed over to Hindi films in the mid-2000s. He was our longest standing brand ambassador, from 2009 to 2016. When I first approached him, he was fresh from the success of *3 Idiots*, the cult film based on Chetan Bhagat's novel *Five Point Someone*. He was a bit foxed when I asked him to become the face of Joyalukkas. Madhavan asked why I was looking for a male brand ambassador, when my clientele was comprised predominantly of women.

We had a long discussion, and he understood where I was coming from. 'A woman wears jewellery to enhance her beauty; to look and feel beautiful. But it is the admiration of others that gives her the validation she needs. It is not the ornaments that are being extolled, but the manner in which she wears them—her choice of jewels, how they complement her attire and the way she carries them off. The jewellery becomes valid only when the person for whom she has embellished herself appreciates their effect—how they enhance her intrinsic beauty. That's what makes the concept so brilliant,' he summed up.

Madhavan liked the fact that we were not 'over-selling'. To quote him again, 'All the other brands are bringing out generic advertisements—glossy visuals of women wearing jewellery. But you can't distinguish one from the other. They all look just the same.'

In Joyalukkas' case, we incorporated stories into the ads. There were 'Moments of Surprise', the 'Joy of Gifting', and so on. Madhavan's absolute favourite was the one that said, 'Heart Says ... Joyalukkas'.

He also commended my insistence on localization—not just in terms of ensuring Joyalukkas' presence in towns, big and small, but hiring 80–90 per cent of the store staff locally. Every time he visited a store, I would insist that he spend some time there, looking at the product offerings, and meeting and greeting the staff and customers. He understood that the walk-through established his association with the brand.

While our campaigns were a cut above the rest, we kept in mind that advertising alone doesn't cut it; you must have something to shout about. The customer is intelligent and will not get taken in by hype. Accordingly, our efforts were geared towards two things: first, establishing a relationship of absolute trust with our customers, and second, making good on the promise that Joyalukkas would add value to their lives.

We also found another customer base, comprising big corporates who were looking for innovative gifting ideas.

B2B: Gold and Glory

The B2B division originated as a marketing concept. We were exploring the idea of direct engagement with customers, through channels other than the mass media. Like everyone else in the gold and jewellery space, we deployed traditional modes of consumer outreach, through print, radio, TV, and billboard advertising. But this involved considerable investment. Could we leverage our vast store network and brand recognition towards organic marketing?

Even as we were ideating, we received an inquiry from the FMCG major Unilever, which has a strong presence in the Middle East. They were looking to promote Lipton Tea in the UAE, by incentivizing small vendors, like tea shops and cafeterias, with some sort of gifts. We came up with the idea of vouchers, in denominations as small as twenty-five dirhams, which could be redeemed at Joyalukkas.

These fungible vouchers were a hit, and drew customers from all parts of the UAE, including places like Fujairah and Umm Al Quwain, where we did not have stores. Our sales staff had been trained to service them, with the result that we acquired a host of new patrons, besides reactivating existing, dormant customers. Unilever had planned to run the campaign for three months, but it was so successful that they extended it by another three months.

The B2B division began in 2003 with a team of two people drawing on the idea of targeting corporations as customers. Our first step was to create brand awareness among corporations, and then understand their requirements. Some of them were looking to incentivize their dealers/distributors, some to conduct promotional campaigns or raffle draws, and others to reward their employees/customers. Having identified their needs, we suggested appropriate products, from vouchers, gold coins and customized gold mementos to co-branding and loyalty tie-ups.

From its very inception, the B2B division understood that the value of gold is not limited to its intrinsic worth, but also lies in its symbolism. Associated with wealth and success, beauty and grandeur, power and generosity, gold imbues any object with a touch of the empyrean. As such, gold lends itself not just to jewellery, but to mementos in any shape and form. Gold is the king among corporate gifts; it evokes positive emotions and makes the recipient feel valued.

I'd followed football avidly as a youth in Kerala, so I was delighted to craft five golden boots for electronics retailer Emax to mark the 2010 FIFA World Cup. As every football fan knows, the Golden Boot and the Ballon d'Or or Golden Ball are much-coveted awards; the former is given to the leading goal scorer in the European leagues and the latter to the player of the year. We created a football shoe in 24-karat gold, complete with cleats, and weighing 650 grams: it was a thing of beauty, and a credit to Joyalukkas' B2B Solutions.

For the 2006 World Cup, we had made fourteen golden footballs for KFC's scratch-and-win promotion across seven countries in the Gulf. Each had the traditional hexagons and pentagons, with one carrying KFC's logo, featuring Colonel Sanders. The multinational came back to us for FIFA World Cup 2014 and commissioned a special memento, an 18-karat plaque in honour of football legend Cristiano Ronaldo.

For us, the potential of a co-branding association is weighed against three parameters: revenue, footfall and branding. Our tie-up with Coca-Cola met all three criteria. The beverage giant is very selective in terms of partnerships, so when it chose to undertake its UTC Promo Campaign–2007 with us, we felt honoured. A representative from Coca-Cola's headquarters in Atlanta visited our office in Dubai, and expressed approval of our processes and market positioning.

They conducted a supplier audit, which basically assesses quality assurance and compliance with industry regulations. In accordance with their global requirements, they also asked us to sign up for their Code of Business Conduct, a set of guidelines on ethical business practices.

The promotion was built around a 'bottle cap' raffle draw. To enter, you bought a Coke bottle and found a number under the cap, which served as a lottery ticket. Coca-Cola agreed to put our logo on the bottle. We provided the prizes: five thousand gold coins of one gram, five grams and ten grams, as well as three diamond necklaces worth ten thousand dollars each. That summer, nearly forty million Coca-Cola bottles in the GCC carried our brand name, and this gave us enormous traction.

For St. Mary's Catholic Church in Dubai, we made commemorative gold coins, and for the Apostolic Vicarate of Southern Arabia, we produced plaques and coins in silver, to mark Pope Francis's first visit to the UAE in 2019, the 'Year of Tolerance'.

In my view, our most spectacular creation was a golden replica of the Burj Khalifa for SanDisk. I think we managed to capture the spirit of the world's tallest building, with subtle serrations marking all its 163 floors.

The B2B division in India focuses on tie-ups with large corporates. In both India and the Gulf, our initiatives in this space have proved successful.

Festival Fever

Our promotions had become a byword in the industry after the Rolls Royce campaign. There was a high demand for BMWs or 'beemer', so I decided they would be the highlight of our 2009 lucky draw, held in the spring. The 'Shop and Drive' event was open to customers around the world and made all the waves we could have hoped for. The following year, we pulled off another 'automotive' coup with our 'Drive your Dream' campaign in India. A Mercedes-Benz E-class car, with its unmatched luxury quotient, was up for grabs in a raffle draw for customers who spent five thousand rupees at our store.

We celebrated every significant festival and continued to come up with something unique to offer our customers. For

Onam, we gave every customer who spent that amount an 'onapuddava', a hand-woven garment with gold brocade.

One of our most successful campaigns was the Akshaya Tritiya promotion of 2005. Shivram Kumar, India director of the WGC, called me out of the blue one day. 'I'm in Dubai, and I have a proposal for your marketing people. Can I meet with them?'

I asked him what it was about, and he replied, 'Akshaya Tritiya'. The festival is celebrated in many parts of India; each region has its own legends and traditions associated with different deities. The one thing in common is that it is regarded as an auspicious day for buying—and gifting—gold and silver. Shivram proposed to leverage that custom to boost sales of gold.

I was curious about his plan and joined my marketing team in a meeting with Shivram, which lasted for two-and-a-half hours. He explained the origin and rationale of his idea in great detail. Shivram told us that back in 2002, he had noticed customers thronging the GRT Jewellery store in Chennai. He went up to the counter and asked the proprietor, G. Rajendran, why there was an unusually large crowd. 'Today is Akshaya Tritiya, an auspicious day to buy gold,' Rajendran told him.

Shivram did some research and found there was a widespread belief that purchasing gold during the Akshaya Tritiya festivities was equivalent to welcoming Lakshmi, the Hindu goddess of wealth, into one's home. For six months, Shivram and his team worked with advertising agencies and newspapers to come up with a solid campaign built around the festival. In 2003, he initiated an advertising campaign in collaboration with four jewellers: NAC, Prince, GRT and

Nathella. They were reluctant at first, because sales of gold during this time were guaranteed in any case. So, the WGC offered to chip in with 25 per cent of the advertising costs.

The campaign was a success, and all the jewellers—even those who hadn't advertised—benefitted. Shivram decided to promote the idea; he was positive that it would trigger massive gold purchases in India and by Indians in the Gulf. He decided to approach me for two reasons. First, he believed I was willing to try new things and had my ear to the ground. Second, we had what no other retailer could offer at the time—a strong store network comprising some forty showrooms in India and the Gulf.

My team and I were enchanted with the idea. It was exactly the kind of campaign we liked, with a strong storyline that we could successfully communicate to potential buyers. My marketing people worked with the WGC for three months to customize the campaign for our constituencies in India and the Gulf. We launched an advertising blitz, with a pre-booking offer publicized through all the prominent TV channels in India and the Gulf. Anyone who booked jewellery worth 1,500 dirhams, or the equivalent in rupees, would get a free ten-gram silver coin embossed with an image of the goddess Lakshmi. On the day, I called Shivram at around 3 p.m. and said, 'I have never seen crowds like this. My stores are jam-packed. I just wanted to thank you for making it possible.'

We went on to do other campaigns with the WGC. From then on, we held a promotion around Akshaya Tritiya every year, both in India and the Gulf. Although Joyalukkas pioneered the concept in the Middle East and in South India, other jewellers soon got on board. Today, Akshaya Tritiya is one of the most prominent festivals on the retail calendar, not only for jewellery, but also for white goods and furniture.

Diamonds with a Difference

Prior to rebranding, I had already launched the 'Joy 145' collection of exclusive diamonds. At the time, diamonds were not part of any jeweller's main production line. Bear in mind that until the turn of the millennium, diamond jewellery comprised a very small percentage of the total market in India and the Gulf.

Customer resistance to diamonds was based on the notion that, unlike gold, they had no resale value. Like a Swarovski figurine, diamonds appealed to aesthetic and aspirational sensibilities, but were not seen as a viable investment.

In the West, diamonds are integral to lifestyle; a proposal of marriage without a diamond ring is unthinkable, and the quality and weight of the stone is a measure of status. South Asia and the Middle East have no such tradition; diamonds are a purely aspirational purchase, and gold remains the first choice when gifting jewellery.

In 2000, De Beers—the best-known name in the diamond industry—had launched its Nakshatra and Asmi range of diamond jewellery in India, supported by a high-visibility campaign featuring Bollywood star Aishwarya Rai. The twin objectives behind the move were to enhance the appeal of diamonds among consumers, and to add value to the product through branding. Some diamond manufacturers took their cue from De Beers and launched their own collections. The Mumbai-based Suashish Diamonds was among them.

Tremendous promotional efforts went into increasing the share of diamond jewellery in the market. Top jewellers guaranteed the product; the consumer could return it to the retailer at any time at the purchase price (minus taxes). Instilling confidence in the consumer went a long way in boosting diamond sales. In fact, very few customers return jewellery, but they need that assurance.

With Suashish, we launched our very first co-branded product, the 'Joy 145' range of brilliant diamonds with dual certification. The standard International Gemological Institute (IGI) certificate refers to the 'four Cs': carat, cut, clarity and colour. The GemEx certificate measures the diamond's brilliance.

The range was not easy to sell; it was 50 per cent more expensive than stones of the same karat weight and clarity, because of the skill and labour that went into the additional facets (145 as compared to 58). The exclusivity of the product was reflected in our ads, which emphasized the sparkle and fire of the solitaires, and the aura they cast around the wearer. Each stone was packaged in an elegant box that had a light within, the better to display its brilliance. It actually did better in India than the Middle East, because consumers back home wanted the very best.

In 2006 we came up with our own range of diamond jewellery, dubbed 'Perfekt'. It was a pioneering product, new to both the Indian and the Middle Eastern markets. The manufacturing process, based on CNC tubing technology, was unknown to jewellers in the region. The technology, used in the manufacture of Swiss watches and automobile components, enabled an incredible precision in the execution of designs, and resulted in pieces that were scratch-proof and corrosion-free, with better lustre and greater strength. What's more, the diamonds set in gold were identical in size and shape. Hence, the name Perfekt.

It was Madhu Dhabuwala, then the sales manager at Jewelex (a sightholder of De Beers), who pitched the idea of the Perfekt collection to me. I immediately saw its potential, and invited her to fly from Dubai to Kochi, where I happened to be at the time. It was a fruitful meeting. While placing the order, I suggested that we should support the product with a mix of marketing campaigns, and a newsworthy launch featuring a celebrity of note.

We worked overtime to put the launch together quickly and smoothly, as I wanted a short time to market. Jewelex agreed to fund half the cost of the launch event, a fashion show in Dubai with Bollywood actor Bhumika Chawla as the face of Perfekt.

We leveraged the 'precision tech' aspect to differentiate the collection from all other product lines. It was unique; it looked and felt international, and yet had an Indian touch. The pieces appeared as classy as those of European jewellers and found favour not only with Indian consumers, but tourists from all over the world, be it the USA, Europe or China. Perfekt was such a hit—even De Beers was highly appreciative of it—that we lost no time in introducing the collection at our stores in India.

In 2010, De Beers launched their premium brand, Forevermark. Engraved on every single stone is an inscription invisible to the naked eye, an assurance to consumers that it meets the highest standards of beauty, rarity and responsible sourcing. According to De Beers, less than 1 per cent of the world's natural diamonds qualify to become part of that exclusive range. When Forevermark approached us for a tie-up, we were happy to do so. It is estimated that by 2030, India will account for 17–18 per cent of the global demand for diamonds.

Awards Galore

In terms of quality, both our processes and products are impeccable, and have always been. As Alukkas Jewellery LLC, we became the first jeweller in the Middle East to obtain ISO 9001:2000 certification in 2004.

Our efforts have brought rewards, in the form of appreciation from both within and outside the industry. An especially proud moment for me was receiving the Dubai Quality Appreciation Programme Award for 2008 from none other than H.H. Sheikh Mohammed Bin Rashid Al Maktoum, vice-president and prime minister of UAE, and ruler of Dubai.

In 2006, I received the local retailer of the year award from H.E. Sheikha Lubna Al Qasimi, then the UAE minister of economy. Joyalukkas was also recognized as the best socially responsible company by prestigious entities both in India and the UAE.

In 2008, for the first time, we recorded an annual turnover of one billion dollars—two years ahead of our target. In 2010, we were recognized as a Superbrand in the Middle East, a title that we would retain for eight years in a row, even as we debuted among the Superbrands in India.

Joyalukkas was one among the prominent global jewellers selected by Forevermark to create masterpieces for the red carpet at the 2016 Oscars. It was a feather in Joyalukkas' cap, and a crowning achievement of the decade 2010–2020, said Sachin Jain, managing director of Forevermark.

All through, we continued to grow based on our reputation for quality and product innovation. We had ambition and imagination, and it was the confluence of the two that led us to the biggest initiative of all—an iconic jewellery store that put the 'extra' in extraordinary.

10

Joy in India

※

Imagine Aladdin's cave, ablaze with gold and gems. Incandescent stacks of treasure meet the eye, a sumptuous visual feast that stretches on and on. Lured into that magical space and engulfed in its golden glow, you feel compelled to explore its wonders.

That sums up the concept of my mega-showroom in Chennai; I conceived it as an unparalleled shopping experience, spread over 51,962 square feet and across four floors, with 1,20,000 jewellery designs to choose from. To enter is to immerse yourself in a dreamscape, where the mundane worries of life no longer exist.

On the day of the inauguration, however, I was a bundle of anxieties.

All that I had built up over the years was riding on the success of the showroom. Virtually everyone I knew—jewellery suppliers, bankers, coworkers, friends and family—had advised against it. The investment in the Chennai store could have funded ten new showrooms; they could not understand why I was putting all my eggs in one gilded basket.

I understood their point of view. Opening ten stores instead of one would have been the safe way to go, increasing the odds of success and reducing the chance of failure. My dream store, on the other hand, entailed a massive capital investment and humongous operating costs. A veritable army of staff had been recruited and trained within an inch of their lives; the interiors had cost a fortune and the stock added up to three-quarters of a tonne of gold. Small wonder my team was concerned about its viability. From a purely financial or investment-model standpoint, it made no sense.

To say that it was an ambitious project was an understatement. At that time, a showroom of respectable size measured 2,000–3,000 square feet, and here I was, thinking twenty-five times bigger. I didn't want just another shop; I wanted the Taj Mahal of showrooms. For most people, fear of failure is a strong deterrent. My greatest fear is mediocrity. Tame acceptance of limitations is not my style; I choose to confront them instead. So, I had made up my mind to enter Chennai with an epic splash, or not at all.

The point is that what appeared impossible to others seemed very possible to me. The time-tested path is not for me; I find my own road. The Chennai store was the latest in a series of examples.

When people ask me 'why', my counter-question is 'why not'. After deciding on a project, I always ask my coworkers and well-wishers to give me reasons not to go ahead. If they are able to present compelling arguments, I reconsider. If not,

I power ahead. In this case, no one was able to fault my rationale. But they were still fearful, because of the sheer scale of the investment involved.

Counterintuitive though it seemed, my reasoning was quite sound. In the highly competitive Chennai market, where brand loyalties are strong, a new entrant would find it difficult to attract customers. To do so, we needed a USP that would make our showroom a must-visit destination. Sheer size, tasteful opulence, and a large and varied inventory would accomplish that objective.

To further pique the customer's interest, I wanted to deploy the concept of experiential shopping. Going to the Chennai showroom ought to be an entertaining day out for our customers and their friends; they should spend as much time as possible in the showroom and leave in good spirits, preferably weighed down with shopping bags!

The site of the showroom was not considered a prime location at the time. Today, the Prashanth Gold Tower building on Usman Road in the 'shopping paradise' of Thyagaraya Nagar (T. Nagar) is a landmark. It is owned by the popular Tamil actor and filmmaker Thiagarajan Sivanandam. As aficionados of Tamil cinema know, it is named after his son, actor–businessman Prashanth Thiagarajan.

It was Thiagarajan who invited me to Chennai. He was deeply interested in jewellery and often attended exhibitions all over the world. One day, he called me with a proposal. 'When I went to Bangkok and Dubai, I was intrigued by the concept of one-stop jewellery stores, with various brands under one roof. So, I thought to myself, why not convert my commercial building in Chennai into a sort of

Gold Souk—a space dedicated to gold jewellery, featuring multiple brands?'

He wanted me to set up a showroom in his building, which was then under construction. I found myself agreeing to visit Chennai to check out the site. When I arrived, I was greeted with much fanfare. It was quite an overwhelming welcome!

Alukkas' history with Chennai was not a happy one. Back in 1990, we had closed our store there after failing to crack the market. At that time, we were operating as a family business and I wasn't in charge, but I felt that we hadn't given it our best shot. Perhaps we should have understood the nuances of the market better; after all, customer buying behaviour, product offerings and the nature of competition varies from region to region. I had taken that failure to heart.

Thiagarajan's offer was an opportunity to erase the past and prove my mettle on the very same territory that Alukkas had ignominiously exited. By this time, we had become 'Joyalukkas'. It was now my business and my brand, so failure was not an option!

When I saw the tower, I was impressed. The ten-storey structure was not ideally located, and the interiors, including the internal wiring and plumbing, had yet to be completed, but I could see that the building had 'good bones'. There were four elevators and an escalator on every floor. Each floor had a twenty-foot ceiling, and the three-level basement had parking space for two hundred cars. It also had a High Definition Power Line Communication, very rare in that part of the city.

After the tour, my mind went into overdrive and I came up with a bold plan. I would hire five floors, the ground floor and the four above, and not merely a shop or a single floor.

Then, I would convert it into a single, massive showroom. The largest in the city, the largest in the country, perhaps even the largest in the world.

A High-Risk Strategy

No sooner had I announced my plans for the Chennai showroom than it came under the intense scrutiny of my competitors. My first step was to convince my close-knit team, so that they bought into my vision. I knew that once they were on board, they would work relentlessly towards the success of the store. As their leader, it was my job to dispel their doubts. It took me some time, but I eventually managed to convince them that the venture was well worth the risk. Finally, they were all on board.

I put Mathews Antony, a dedicated member of my team, in charge of the Chennai store. The interiors were entrusted to in-house designer Hemant Shinde. From the start, I had surmised that the construction work would prove very challenging.

In the eighteen months prior to the opening of the mega-showroom, I must have made around thirty trips to Chennai. My team was under immense pressure, as reworking the layout of an existing structure to meet our requirements was more complicated than starting from scratch.

The internal wiring, plumbing and air conditioning were yet to be done, besides which the approval of various regulatory agencies, like the fire department, had to be obtained. It was daunting, but we accomplished it, without bending any rules.

Reconstructing the upper floors was a delicate task, because we had to ensure that the structural integrity of the foundations and the building itself were maintained. There was no rule book at my disposal, so I had to rely on my own ingenuity (most of my creative pursuits have had happy outcomes, and I have always treated the occasional failure as part of the learning curve).

I took great care in designing the interiors, because I was aiming at a five-star ambience; I wanted the entire store to have a luxurious feel. To that end, I had ordered a massive, customized boat-shaped crystal chandelier from Dubai, with about a thousand light bulbs!

The fit-out of the showroom took about fifteen months, given that it was ten times as large as any of my other outlets. The problem of insurance also cropped up. Insurers balked at the prospect of a huge volume of high-value inventory parked in a single location. The risk was too great, they felt. Security was a major area of concern, as a store of that size was vulnerable to shop-lifters and burglars. So, we were wrestling with problems on various fronts. Then came the biggest challenge of all.

The economic crisis of 2008, a 'Black Swan' event, cast its dark shadow over my dream project. By February of that year, the collapse of mortgage-backed securities had dealt a severe blow to financial institutions in the USA, signalling an impending global recession. Gold prices doubled, as they do in times of crisis.

Any increase in the price of gold puts huge pressure on the sales and cash flow of a jewellery business. All at once, the viability of our mammoth venture was called into question. The bigger the project, the bigger the risk. So, our bankers shied away and refused to put up the funds. My strenuous efforts to persuade them were in vain.

Fortunately, jewellery wholesalers were more accommodating. My strict insistence on timely payments to our suppliers had given us great credibility in the market. Thanks to this reputation for reliability, we were able to procure stock on credit. Bear in mind that wholesalers extend short-term credit, of up to thirty days. Given that ours was a long-term project, this was obviously not sustainable. So why had I had taken the one-month credit route?

The answer lay in the high-risk strategy I had conceived. I would take stock on credit and open the store. Its spectacular success would convince bankers of its viability, and they would sanction the funds. I could then pay off my creditors. I was supremely confident of the project's potential, but I had to demonstrate it for the benefit of our bankers. What if I were wrong? I refused to consider the possibility; 'what ifs' have never been part of my lexicon.

There was another hitch in the plan: our suppliers insisted on supplying jewellery at a fixed price. This was not the normal practice. Usually, credit was given on an unfixed basis, which means that the price of gold supplied to the jeweller is not predetermined. On the due date, payment is made in gold equal to the quantity procured, along with the making charges. The wholesaler has an identical arrangement with the manufacturers and they, in turn, with the bullion banks.

This back-to-back arrangement between all the stakeholders hedges against fluctuation in the price of gold. Everyone is protected. It also means that jewellers don't make a profit on an increase in gold prices. Nor do they suffer a loss when prices fall.

This time, the suppliers wanted to provide jewellery on a fixed basis. Gold was at a peak, offering them an opportunity to make windfall gains before prices fell. The entire trade was convinced that the gold price would follow historic trends, and as was the case in 1980, the peak would be followed by a spectacular crash.

If I procured jewellery on a fixed basis, and the bottom fell out of the gold market, I would be incurring huge losses. Wisdom lay in postponing the inauguration of the showroom, otherwise, I might find myself in a financial crisis.

I decided to open the showroom. My team was deeply perturbed, as were my friends in the industry. To a man, they advised me strongly against the move. But I went ahead and procured 750 kilograms of gold on a fixed-price basis.

It may have come across as a rash decision, but it was backed by solid reasoning. I don't claim to be an expert in forecasting gold prices, but like any other businessman, I keep track of trends. The price of gold in rupees has always followed an upward trend, one reason being the slow but steady weakening of the Indian rupee against the US dollar.

I inferred that since India was a developing economy, this upward trajectory would continue for the next few decades. The price of gold would rise in the medium to long term, regardless of short-term hiccups. Relying on my intuition, I went ahead with my plans. I can't say it was an easy decision, but once it was made, there was no going back.

The Inauguration

In mid-2007, when the project was halfway through, I announced the date of inauguration: 16 March 2008. I had selected the date carefully, to coincide with Akshaya Tritiya, the best possible time to capture the market. To expedite the project, we had around a thousand people working round the clock in different shifts. In no time at all, word spread across the industry, and our competitors, suppliers and bankers turned up to take a sneak peek at the upcoming showroom.

The majority of those involved with the project were doubtful that it could be completed on time, and advised me to postpone the inauguration. I turned a deaf ear, and added more people to the workforce. By early March 2008, it became clear that we would be able to adhere to the declared date.

Finding accommodation for our four hundred–strong store staff near the showroom was a challenge. We hired a three-star hotel on a long-term lease and fitted the entire building with air-conditioners, so that my staff would be at ease in Chennai's tropical climate. I decided to appoint Mathews as the head of the store, because he had done an excellent job during the fit-out. He was to be assisted by five managers, one on each floor.

To set the stage for the grand inauguration, we conducted a massive door-to-door direct marketing campaign across a major part of Chennai city, inviting people to the event. Beautifully crafted invitations were distributed. Additional publicity was generated through an advertising blitz explaining the concept of the larger-than-life showroom, with eye-catching visuals of some of our iconic pieces of jewellery. The ads were placed in movie theatres and newspapers, and on massive hoardings. We also put up the giant flexes for which Chennai is known. It was the biggest ever inaugural campaign in jewellery retail.

On 15 March, our back-end team was asked to undertake the finishing touches and then vacate all five floors for the unboxing of 1,20,000 pieces of jewellery. Our carefully curated product range had been sourced from all parts of India, as well as Italy, Singapore and Turkey. Four hundred members of the Chennai store staff, as well as senior managers from our other stores, were assigned to verify each piece and enter the particulars into the enterprise resource planning (ERP) system, before putting it on display. The entire process took sixteen hours. I will be forever grateful to my team for having pulled it off successfully, and on time.

The following day, my dream store opened its doors to the world. Diplomats, industrialists, cine stars, media persons and members of the public converged on Usman Road in their thousands for the event. The who's who of Chennai were present, many of whom I had personally invited, along with prominent NRIs.

Surjit Singh Barnala, then the governor of Tamil Nadu, inaugurated the showroom. The gold section was unveiled by Philip Oldan, managing director (marketing and jewellery) of the World Gold Council, and the diamond section by Roland Lorie, CEO of the International Gemological Institute in Antwerp, Belgium.

The prelaunch publicity had been widespread, right from the day Thiagarajan and I announced the project, to the eve of the opening. As expected, the inauguration made waves in the media, especially in the pink papers. Joyalukkas became the cynosure of all eyes; well-wishers and detractors alike waited with bated breath for the outcome. Would the mega-showroom flop and reduce my company to financial rubble, or would it succeed and set a new trend in jewellery retail?

From Day One, the Chennai store was a triumph. Customers poured in, to the point that we had to station over a dozen security guards to manage the crowds. Some came to shop, others simply to enjoy the ambience. My decision to power through the global financial crisis–induced chaos had been vindicated.

I had made sure that the top executives from our banks attended the inaugural function and witnessed the crowd response firsthand. The result: within a few weeks of the opening, the banks released the funds I had asked for.

Three years later, in March 2011, the *Limca Book of Records* declared Joyalukkas, T. Nagar, as the largest gold jewellery showroom in the world, a record yet to be broken. Footfall increased steadily and in a surprisingly short time, we became the go-to jewellery destination for celebrities, politicians and businessmen from across India, a fact that attracted even more customers.

A brief description of the store is in order. The ground floor is dedicated entirely to gold jewellery catering to a variety of tastes, from lighter pieces for daily wear to antique and temple jewellery.

The first floor showcases gemstone-studded precious jewellery. On the second floor, patrons can find diamond jewellery, solitaires and uncut diamonds. On the third floor is our silver collection, comprising ornaments, tableware, statuettes, candelabras and so on.

On the fourth floor is the Diamond Cave, a first-of-its-kind innovation that attracts a large number of visitors. Designed to look like an actual cave, it showcases the process of making diamond jewellery, from start to finish. Patrons take the journey from mines to hearts, and learn how diamonds are sourced, cut and polished, and finally set in precious metals. Schoolchildren and college students are frequent visitors. The fifth floor is dedicated to the back office.

We have separate sections for wedding jewellery and gift items, including designer watches. A gemstone consultant is at hand to answer any queries the customer might have. The showroom also has a design studio for bespoke jewellery.

Another innovation is a children's play area, which contributes to a relaxed shopping experience. In addition, we have ensured comfortable seating arrangements, so that shoppers can get off their feet for a while. The staff has been trained to receive and attend to customers with courtesy and patience. The idea is to make shopping as relaxing and enjoyable as possible.

When I look back at the tough decisions I had to take to make the store possible, I experience a quiet sense of satisfaction. I must mention that at the time of writing, the price of gold is 200 per cent higher than it was when the Chennai store opened. My assessment of the gold price trend has proved to be correct. The main takeaway from this is that action is better than inaction. Only then can a solution emerge.

The Chennai store was a landmark event in Joyalukkas' journey; it catapulted us into the big league. We were no longer just another regional player. In a couple of years, my competitors began opening large-sized showrooms, but I like to think that ours is still head and shoulders above the rest.

In Tamil Nadu, India's biggest gold-consuming state after Kerala, I opened stores in Salem, Tirunelveli, Madurai, Thanjavur, Karur, Vellore and Kanchipuram. Chennai, of course, was the Kohinoor in our crown. And then came two showrooms very close to my heart: one at my hometown, Thrissur, and another in the state capital, Thiruvananthapuram. Subsequently, we also debuted in India's IT capital, Bengaluru, with a massive showroom spread across four floors, and in Mumbai, the financial heart of India and home of Bollywood.

Over time, we found that once we had opened our store in a particular location, it became something of a landmark in the city, and a hub for markets.

Show Me the Money

In this tale of exponential expansion, one question has remained unanswered: who put up the money? Obviously, the rapid proliferation of Joyalukkas stores called for deep pockets. That is a story in itself, one in which chance, strategic thinking, an alignment of interests and the sheer bullheadedness of the protagonist (me) all played a part. The starring role, however, was that of ABN Amro Bank.

I have mentioned that banks were wary of lending to jewellers. A case in point was the Bank of Baroda. They had a branch in Dubai, and I had a current account there. It was the only banking relationship I had, so one fine day I walked into the manager's office and asked for a loan.

I wanted to scale up my business. From early 2000 onwards, it was clear to me that the jewellery market in the Gulf was poised to grow spectacularly. Dubai had been positioned as the City of Gold, and demand was escalating, thanks to the increasing expatriate population. The all-round development of Dubai as a global hub had drawn both skilled and unskilled workers from South Asia. Besides, profitability had improved owing to the Board Rate margin.

But I needed capital. At the time, a single store needed an investment of US$1.5–2 million, most of it in stock, and the rest for the fit-out and interiors. Today, that figure would be closer to ten million dollars. While Yusuf Nunu had supported me with working capital credit, my expansion plans were beyond his means.

So, I approached the Bank of Baroda. As usual, we had deposited our cash collections that morning—a tedious exercise that involved two staffers doing the rounds of all our Dubai stores to pick up the money, recounting it and then taking it to the bank. Invariably, there would be a long queue, as all the traders in the Gold Souk had their accounts in the Deira branch of the Bank of Baroda.

The bank was not inclined to extend a loan. The manager heard me out, and then told me that I would have to park one million dirhams with the bank, in order to get a credit of 1.1 million dirhams. 'A fixed deposit of one million dirhams, at an interest of 3 per cent, will be your collateral. Against that, we will give you an overdraft facility of 1.1 million dirhams, at 5 per cent per annum,' he said.

It didn't take a genius to figure out that he was proposing a very bad deal. As soon as I emerged from the bank, I gave instructions to close our account there. We shifted to the Habib AG Zurich bank, but they didn't offer me any credit either. The only advantage was that the manager ensured a separate window for cash deposits, so that my staff was spared the long wait in a queue.

The funding issue remained unresolved. And then, I had an unexpected stroke of good fortune. It turned out that what I had been seeking was seeking me too.

In early 2002, I ran into a couple of officials from the ABN Amro Bank at a jewellery exhibition. I knew that they were leading financiers of the diamond trade, and had regional offices in Antwerp, New York, Hong Kong and Mumbai. They would doubtless have opened one in Thrissur, if diamond cutting and polishing had not moved to Surat in the late 1950s!

I learnt that they had recently set up an office in Dubai, and were looking to on-board credible clients to grow their books. So, Freddy Hanard, who headed ABN Amro's operations in the Middle East, Europe and Africa, and Harjit Singh, the Dubai head, dropped in at my office in the Gold Land building to which we had shifted in 2000 (moving to a much larger corporate office space had become necessary, because the rapid growth of our retail outlets demanded a highly organized and resourceful back office).

I had departmentalized the company. In addition to the procurement and accounts departments, we added marketing, finance, HR, internal audit and so on. All of them were formally structured, with roles clearly demarcated. I recruited Renjith C.P., who had worked with Madco Gulf and the Dubai Gold and Jewellery Group, to serve as general manager of my company. The office was the headquarters of our international operations and housed all our departments.

The visit by ABN Amro, I realized, was a smell test, geared towards understanding the background of the company, and its management style and processes. Direct interaction with the promoter is imperative in understanding his business; it tells you what reports and numbers do not. Freddy and Harjit were impressed with our team and structure, and even more so with my vision for growth. They also did a recce of some of our stores.

They got back to me promptly, stating that my growth story was compelling, and they were willing to put up the funds for expansion. Our numbers were audited by KPMG, a fact that enhanced our credibility.

In a very short space of time, we received credit approval from Antwerp, and ABN sanctioned a credit limit of five million dollars. A few months later, HSBC extended us a credit facility of up to 10,000 ounces of gold. All at once, two international banks were on board. Smaller banks followed, piggybacking on the larger banks.

The trouble was that I had zero capital to commence business in India. We had been opening store after store in the Gulf, which absorbed all our profits. By this time, our funding from the banks totalled around ten million dollars, a figure which fell short of our growth capital requirement. We were also bound by banking covenants which forbade us from withdrawing funds from the business.

As always, I had powered ahead in India without committed funding. I don't usually have a plan on the drawing board; I just decide on a target and plan backwards. As a result, I was left high and dry.

Desperate times call for desperate measures, so I withdrew fifty crore rupees from our Dubai entity. It served as seed capital for our stores in Kerala, first in Kottayam, followed by Angamaly, Thodupuzha and Thiruvalla.

The issue of fund constraints remained, as none of the Kerala-based banks were willing to extend credit to me. One after another, they declined our proposal, saying that they did not have a 'credit appetite for jewellers'. As for our banks in Dubai, they could not assist us as India was outside their purview. ABN Amro, which had its regional office in Mumbai, was the exception. Harjit and I flew to the bank's global headquarters in Antwerp to meet Freddy and his boss, ABN Amro CEO Peter Grosh. Both seemed interested in a long-term relationship and asked me several questions about Alukkas' history.

Having secured the support of ABN Amro's top officials, we met the bank's Asia regional head, Biju Patnaik, in Mumbai. I found him a thorough gentleman, with an eye for revenue. His bank funded diamantaires, but didn't regard retailers as a viable proposition. He was curious about me for two reasons: first, because standalone stores were the norm in those days, and second, I was heading to India from Dubai, a reversal of the usual trend.

I told him my story and shared my plans for India, explaining that we had a unique business model in mind. Our Wedding Centre would bring jewellery, textiles and various accessories under one roof. The positioning made sense, I explained, as half of the total demand for jewellery in India is wedding-related. He liked the idea. Harjit was dispatched for a detailed onsite report, and he visited all our stores in Kerala. Needless to say, his report was positive.

The eight new stores planned for the next two years involved an outlay of seventy crore rupees—fifty crore for inventory and the rest for the fit-outs. In mid-2003, Antwerp green-lighted the proposal and put up fifty crore rupees. The rest was managed on medium-term credit from suppliers. I began hunting for locations.

Biju personally visited our Kochi office once in three months to prepare quarterly reports. We were the bank's first retail client in India, so he wanted to know all about hedging gold, inventory management and systems for controlling the flow of high-value goods and cash. We learnt from each other.

By 2006, ABN Amro had realized that their funding alone could not support our growth trajectory, so Biju formed a consortium of four banks and increased funding to hundred crore rupees. We continue to grow exponentially with more and more prominent banks joining in. Meanwhile, access to bank credit had gradually improved for the jewellery sector as a whole.

A point to be noted is that I didn't block my capital in real estate. Most of my shops were on rent. However, our appetite for funds grew as we sought to scale the business. On the strength of our brand, we received funding proposals that seemed prima facie very attractive. But there's no such thing as unconditional funding. I had to examine the offers carefully and take tough decisions. For I realized that not all money is the same.

11

Prelude to an IPO

Rakesh Jhunjhunwala looked at me intently through his rimless spectacles, as if he were sizing me up. I wondered what exactly did India's biggest bull want from me. The man was a legend—an investor with an uncanny knack for picking winners, a stock trader who could move markets and a deal-maker par excellence. I had heard that he'd started his journey as an investor with five thousand rupees and ended up in Forbes' as one of the 500 richest individuals in the world.

For almost three hours, he and his team had sought to evaluate our operational metrics—financial, marketing, distribution, production, sales, store economics and so on. Sure of our ground, we answered every question without hesitation. From the inquisition emerged the picture of a robust company, a veritable model of financial health. In addition, we had a presence spanning the globe, a solid customer base and a substantial market share both in India and overseas.

The meeting had been set up by my long-time associate, Shailesh Sangani, founder of Priority Jewels. He had called me in breathless excitement, saying, 'Joy, Rakesh Jhunjhunwala would like to meet you, regarding an investment in Joyalukkas.'

Shailesh was a well-wisher of mine, a stalwart of the industry and a gentleman with great zest for life. I had first met him in 1999, when he had visited the Alukkas store in Thrissur. Several years later, I gave him a massive order and we had been friends ever since. He was known for his infectious high spirits and intimate knowledge of what was happening within the industry, which he was always happy to share with me. So, when he called me in November 2019, I immediately accepted his offer of setting up a meeting with the uncrowned king of Dalal Street (a metonymy for India's financial markets).

Such was Jhunjhunwala's reputation that he had only to express his interest in a company for its share price to rise. I was both intrigued and flattered by his desire to meet with me. Half-a-dozen questions were running through my mind. Should I sell a stake in my company? How much was I willing to part with? Was the timing correct, or should I wait? What kind of valuation could I hope for? To what extent would it help, when I went forward with an Initial Public Offering (IPO)? And most of all, was I emotionally prepared for such a step?

We met at the Rare Enterprises premises in Mumbai's Nariman Point (the city's original central business district) some two weeks later, on 25 November 2019. As we entered his imposing office, the first words that entered my head were 'big bull', because there were statuettes and sculptures of bulls scattered all around the room! I was also struck by the back-to-back screens, which enabled him to monitor his investments in real time.

Clad in a comfortable loose shirt and pants, he was ensconced in a swivel chair and turned around to greet us. He introduced us to his research team and to Mithun Sacheti, co-founder of the online jewellery retailer CaratLane (a subsidiary of the Titan Company), who was also present. On Shailesh's advice, I had brought two of my colleagues with me: Baby George, CEO of Joyalukkas India Ltd, and Nandakumar, who was our chief financial officer at the time. We took our places around a large table and the meeting began. They got down to business at once. We were well-prepared and had all the numbers on our fingertips. At the end of it, Jhunjhunwala pronounced himself deeply impressed with our company's performance, particularly the fact that our operating expenses were one of the lowest in the industry. He was also curious about me and my background.

Jhunjhunwala's objective became clear to me. He believed Joyalukkas would add tremendous value to any entity that chose to invest in us. Our brand identity was established globally; we were strong in South India and had a foothold in international markets. Thus, we were capable of offering real growth in sales. Joyalukkas was a bridge brand between the masses and the premium market. From his perspective, it made perfect sense.

If I acquiesced to the acquisition, our combined cash profit for that year would be added to the investor's kitty, which would translate into an expansion of shareholders' value from day one. From every angle, we were a potential goldmine. For Rakesh Jhunjhunwala the investor, the value creation post listing, in terms of the new price discovery resulting in a higher market capitalization, would have been substantial.

After the meeting, we headed to the ITC Maratha, where we were staying. A short while later, Jhunjhunwala's representative showed up with an offer. He asked if we would consider diluting our interest to the extent of 60 per cent. We were taken aback, because prior to the meeting, the idea of parting with a controlling interest in the company had not even occurred to us. All we had discussed among ourselves was the potential advantage of Jhunjhunwala investing in our company, if we went public. An association with 'India's Warren Buffett' would be prestigious in itself, we felt, and would help us market the issue more aggressively.

We gave Jhunjhunwala's associate a non-committal reply. Later that evening, the Joyalukkas team had dinner with Shailesh at the hotel. It was he who clarified the matter. The company in question was interested in an initial 60 per cent stake, and would eventually buy us out completely or convert our holdings into shares. The Joyalukkas brand would become part of a large corporate entity. He pointed out that we stood to make windfall gains. I could retire and spend more time with my grandchildren in Dubai!

I had a critical decision to make. To sell or not to sell? For me, it was a no-brainer.

A Sweet and Sour PE Story

It was not the first time that I had considered a private equity (PE) investment in Joyalukkas. Back in 2007, when Joyalukkas was on the cusp of an expansion spree, I had decided to raise growth capital through a private placement to potential investors.

By that time, we had thirty-three stores in the Gulf and twelve in India. Our growth mirrored that of the 'City of Gold'. Dubai had embarked on its own rebranding exercise and was moving away from a trade-based economy to a tourism- and services-oriented one. Tourism had triggered a real estate and construction boom. The Burj Khalifa was coming up, the artificial island of Palm Jumeirah had taken shape, the Dubai Science Park had opened its doors to biotech companies, and the Dubai Waterfront was under development. Transport was one of the main drivers of the economy, as was the trade in gold and diamonds.

Dubai, my home away from home, was growing in double digits, and I was determined to accelerate Joyalukkas' growth as well. My objective was to have a hundred stores by the end of 2010, at least fifty of them in the Gulf. To fund rapid expansion of that scale, we needed an infusion of at least one hundred million dollars. The trouble was that no bank, or consortium, had the bandwidth to provide that level of funding at the time.

Hence, the idea of a private placement of equity, with each of two or three investors acquiring a 10 to 15 per cent stake in Joyalukkas' business in the Gulf. I was very clear that the maximum dilution should not exceed a 30 per cent share in the company. Keeping this in view, I appointed two consulting firms: KPMG to identify investors, and PricewaterhouseCoopers (PwC) to undertake the valuation of our business in the Gulf. The latter, after a rigorous exercise of due diligence, came up with the figure of three hundred million dollars for our Gulf business.

Sharad Bandari, then partner and head of transaction services at KPMG, helped us scrutinize the list of potential investors, and we homed in on Arcapita, an investment bank headquartered in Bahrain. An exclusive agreement was signed with them on 19 July 2007. It looked as if we were on course to a PE placement. The process kicked off with the visit of the Arcapita bank team, led by its director of corporate investments, Jonathan Squires, to our corporate office in the Gold Land building, Dubai.

An in-house team was there to welcome them and answer all their questions. We also gave them a tour of our flagship showroom in Dubai. They appeared to be very pleased with what they saw and heard. Squires turned to me and said, 'Mr Joy, please help us understand your India operations.' I promptly invited them to visit India, and just as quickly, they accepted. Supported by a carefully selected team, I personally received them in Kochi.

The tour began with a meeting at our corporate office, followed by visits to several of our stores in Kerala. They were intrigued by the fact that the Indian market was highly fragmented. Organized retail was still a work in progress and no family-owned jeweller—other than us—had a corporate management structure overseeing operations. That's what set us apart, and impressed the Arcapita team. Our last stop was the Coimbatore store, then the largest in India in terms of size and revenue. I flew Squires and his associates there in my private plane.

I had bought the aircraft for two reasons. The first was my fascination with engineering, be it automobiles, planes or construction. In 1999, I attended an air show in Dubai, and was captivated by the small aircraft used for short-haul business travel. I pitched the idea of buying a plane to my brothers, but they shot it down.

The second and far more important reason was utilitarian. While expanding in India, I realized that having an aircraft at my disposal would allow me to visit existing stores and scout sites for new stores in multiple cities in a day, thereby saving a lot of time. And in business, time is money. Initially, I leased an aircraft, but as the frequency of my travels increased, I found that availability was often an issue, so I decided to purchase the same model of aircraft that I had leased, that is, the P.68C Turbo with a propeller engine. It was efficient and economical, particularly for short-haul flights from city to city. I was informed by the manufacturer, Vulcanair of Italy, that I would have to wait for over a year for a new aircraft. So, I decided to buy a pre-owned aircraft from a European who was looking to sell.

The tour gave the Arcapita team an insight into the Indian customer's large appetite for gold and the massive purchasing power of the middle class. In short, I could not have given them a better idea of Joyalukkas' enormous potential and the benefits of partnering with us. I waited for their response with mounting anticipation. They did not keep me waiting for too long. On 3 September, I received an email from Squires. It read: 'Dear Joy, I wanted to summarize where Arcapita is in its thinking regarding an investment in your company. It goes without saying that we remain very interested in partnering with you and we believe strongly that Arcapita can add value to Joyalukkas by bringing our considerable experience in building companies and expanding their reach.'

Then came the googly. Arcapita wanted a 50.1 per cent stake internationally and a 10 per cent stake in India. They also wanted minority protection rights, that is, seats on our board, corporate governance requirements and approval for policy decisions with veto power. Further, they wanted an assurance that I would spend more time on the development of our business in the Gulf.

Over the next fortnight, Squires and his team spared no effort to bring us on board. They sought to reassure me that the minority protection rights would not deprive me of agency in my own company. He also offered to introduce me to the CEOs of major retailers like Caribou and Bijoux Terner, where Arcapita had invested, so that I could understand their style of working.

Frankly, I was truly astounded by the proposal, although I did not react visibly. At no stage had I contemplated parting with a majority stake in my company. I wanted to position Joyalukkas on the gold map of the world, but not at the cost of losing control of the business. My objective was to take the company public at some point in the future, and enable a clear exit for PE investors at that stage. I was not going to sell out my legacy at any price.

Arcapita had the capital I needed. They had the financial muscle to actualize my expansion plans. But I had the power to say no. I refused to accept the deal.

After several days of introspection in the wake of the Arcapita episode, I decided to abandon my plan of courting PE investments, and concentrate on organic growth. By 2015, I was immensely grateful that I had stuck to my guns. My patience had paid off, and the valuation of our Dubai company had increased by a factor of three. I had accomplished my goals, without surrendering my legacy.

To this day, the valuation report of 2007 sits in my office, reminding me that self-belief and aspiration are more valuable than resources.

Finding Funding

Having decided against the PE option, I was back to square one. The question of where I would get the funds for my proposed expansion remained unanswered.

Most companies opt for a mix of debt and equity financing. Each has its drawbacks and advantages. The key differentiators are ownership, control and costs. The manifest advantage of equity financing is that there's no repayment obligation and capital is available for the long term, to fuel growth. On the other hand, it means giving up a portion of ownership and control. I was not ready for that, even if it meant an additional financial burden on the company. To my mind, Joyalukkas had a lot to achieve as a single-owner entity, before bringing in outside investors.

The Arcapita experience had hardened my determination to retain independence and control of the business, which was more valuable to me than stacks of money. If you have the drive and the commitment, and a clear-cut goal backed by an execution strategy, resources will materialize.

Bankers do not tell you how to run the business or what strategies to follow; their sole concern is the security of their investment and timely repayment. So, bank debt—although it comes with certain conditions—does not curb independent decision-making. I instructed my finance team to look into bank funding options.

In July 2008, they received a tempting offer from the BNP Paribas branch in Dubai. The draft term sheet from the bank indicated that they were willing to syndicate a borrowing limit of one hundred million dollars for our company. I was astounded and excited. It would be our biggest single borrowing so far, enough to bankroll twenty new stores in the Gulf.

At once, I began recalibrating my expansion plans to take advantage of the windfall. While I identified locations for new stores, my finance team worked on the funding deal. In terms of the lending assessment, we ticked all the boxes: the character of the entrepreneur (yours truly), the capacity of our business and the conditions we agreed upon. We were on course to finalize the deal. Unfortunately, we hadn't counted on the fourth 'C'—the crisis of 2008.

The global financial crisis that was threatening to derail our store in Chennai also torpedoed our deal with BNP Paribas. Financial institutions across the globe suffered severe damage, beginning with the collapse of Lehman Brothers. Liquidity dried up, and risk appetite was dramatically curtailed. Gold as a secured asset was at an all-time high. BNP Paribas backed out of the deal as market conditions turned adverse, and my expansion plans were put on the backburner once again.

Inured to the proverbial unpredictability of the world of business, I did not waste time in regrets. Instead, I focused my energies on India, which had been left virtually untouched by the great recession that affected the Organization for Economic Cooperation and Development (OECD) economies and parts of the Middle East, particularly the UAE. We went into an expansion overdrive in India, even as we soldiered on through the slowdown in the Gulf.

The world bounced back from the financial crisis. Over the next decade, opportunities for business burgeoned, creating scope for expansion in the Gulf. For instance, we had been contemplating an entry into the Kingdom of Saudi Arabia for a long time. Given its huge expatriate population and sizable geography, the country offered many possibilities for our business, but we did not have a suitable partner.

One day, my compatriot from Thrissur and chairman and managing director of the Lulu Group, Yusuff Ali M.A., put forward a suggestion: 'Joy, I am opening the first Lulu Hypermarket in Al Khobar in KSA. You should open a jewellery store there.'

All at once, I had been offered a gateway to the Saudi market. I lost no time in sending Henry George, who was then my retail manager, on a reconnaissance trip. He has been with us since 1999, graduating from sales to heading challenging projects like identifying and renovating stores. Henry came back with a positive report. In 2011, we opened our first store in Al Khobar. Over time, Saudi Arabia became an excellent market for our international operations.

Entering a new market requires funding. For a jewellery business, raising funds from banks was never simple, let alone long-term borrowings. Most banks only lend short-term funds, usually working capital for a year conditional upon an annual review, with renewal subject to their discretion. Committing to a long-term project with short-term funds is always fraught with risk in terms of liquidity and continuity of the business.

According to the lending norms, we required collateral to be eligible for long-term borrowings, in the form of tangible assets like land and buildings or a high value inventory. However, our business in the Gulf did not own anything by way of real estate, and pledging/hypothecating gold was discouraged under Sharia, the legal code derived from the Holy Quran.

We had to come up with an innovative security structure acceptable to lenders. So, our finance team, headed by Thomas Scaria, proposed that point of sale (POS) collections could be structured as security. Like most jewellers, we were highly liquid. With digitization, card payments had replaced cash sales, resulting in greater throughput; that is, the amount of money circulated through the bank. We pitched the idea to several lenders, and in February 2012, after a few months of deliberation, three major banks came forward to support our growth plans.

The consortium led by Standard Chartered bank agreed to a five-year term loan of one hundred million dollars through a syndication. The much-needed infusion of capital enabled us to strengthen our branch network in KSA, and enter new markets like Singapore and Malaysia where competition was virtually non-existent at the time.

Finding a suitable location for our store in Singapore was extremely challenging. My son, John Paul, volunteered to visit the island country to scout for a location. He had formally joined the company as a management trainee in 2007, after obtaining his Bachelor of Business Administration degree from Manipal University's Dubai campus. For the first year, I did not give him a salary. When he raised the issue with me, I said, 'Salary is for employees.' Then I gave him a supplementary credit card for his expenses! In retrospect, it was a good move, because he learnt financial discipline. In 2010, he became executive director, and steadily worked his way up to become managing director of Joyalukkas' international operation by 2021.

John visited Singapore's 'Little India', which lies to the east of the Singapore river, to look for a site on the main commercial thoroughfare, Serangoon Road. It is dominated by the Mustafa Centre, a retail hub that has long been a must-see for South Asian tourists. He discovered that historically, any shops that opened beyond the Mustafa Centre failed within three years, because customer footfall ended there!

John decided that Joyalukkas would buck the trend. He found a location beyond the Mustafa Centre that perfectly met our requirements in terms of space, window display and signage. We sealed the deal, and within a short space of time, opened our doors. Indian-origin Singaporeans recognized the brand and began to frequent the store. Footfall increased rapidly, so much so that other stores opened alongside Joyalukkas, to take advantage of the growing traffic.

Along with Southeast Asia, we were keen on a presence in North America. The POS security structure had proved effective and efficient for both the lenders and the client. We replicated the model in 2015, when we needed capital to support our expansion in the USA. This time around, we increased the loan by a factor of 1.5, that is, to five hundred million dirhams. Our innovative funding structure won the award for the 'Best Regional Structured Trade Finance Solution' at the 2016 Asset Asian Awards (AAA) in Hong Kong.

The support of banks has always aided the expansion of my business. But with great borrowings, comes great responsibility. That sense of accountability has kept me grounded. I have never lost focus or allowed myself to be distracted by extraneous opportunities. Over three-and-a-half decades in business, I have seen many entrepreneurs default on payments and court bankruptcy, all through reckless borrowing to fund speculative ventures outside of their core business.

I have never bought into investment advice that calls for parking profits elsewhere as a safety net. For me, my business is the safest place to invest my profits, and I draw on them in times of need. That's my Plan A, and it's my one and only plan. There's no Plan B. As my father once told me, 'If you know your business and manage your funds in a responsible manner, then it is alright to borrow.'

To IPO or Not to IPO?

In 2011, I seriously considered going public. We appointed financial experts, drew up a draft prospectus and received the necessary approvals. At the eleventh hour, I withdrew. My instincts told me that the time was not ripe for an IPO. Several people had advised me against it.

My daughter, Mary, who had returned from the UK after a one-year M.Sc. programme in international business, was one of them. She was working on her dissertation at the time, and we held long discussions on various aspects of business, like acquisitions and mergers and the importance of company hierarchies and processes. I asked her to join the IPO roadshow and took her with me to Mumbai to meet potential investors.

At the meeting, we were grilled by investors on our business. They went into the minutiae of our valuation, growth and so on. Many of the questions were very specific, and we had answers to most of them, but not all. Afterwards, Mary observed that we were perhaps not quite ready for that kind of cross-examination. It was an eye-opener for us. So, I began to rethink our preparedness for an IPO.

There were other reasons as well. One was that it would bring us under the purview of regulatory bodies and attract a lot of unnecessary attention from the media. Another institutional investor who attended the IPO roadshow pointed out that with banks willing to provide adequate funding, an IPO was not required at the time. The fact is that I had a goal in mind, a minimum target that I wanted to achieve before going public.

Fast forward to 2019, and the offer from Rakesh Jhunjhunwala (who, sadly, passed away in 2022). My heart was against the deal, and so was my head. John Paul was of the opinion that we should not act hastily. He felt that there was no harm in pursuing the matter further and getting a clearer view of its implications, but without making a commitment of any kind. After all, it was an opportunity to become bigger.

For me, there was a strong emotional element involved. The company and I had a shared identity; it bore my name, and in a very real way, was an extension of myself. I was simultaneously the steward of my father's legacy and the founder of its new avatar. Naturally, my primary concern was how the future of the company would shape up in hands other than my own.

I gave the matter serious thought. From 2001 onwards, we had experienced sustained growth. Without diluting equity, we had entered the big league and built a strong brand. I felt no need to leapfrog into the stratosphere on the shoulders of others. I would get there, but on my own steam.

Whatever happened, I did not want to surrender control of the company, or have managers looking over my shoulder at all times. Yes, it would increase my wealth many times over, but beyond a point, the number of zeroes in your bank balance do not matter. I had enough money for my family's needs; having more would not change the quality of our lives. So once again, I said 'no' to money!

India, at the start of the 2020s, was an exciting market. The economy was on a growth spurt, middle-class incomes had risen, more youth were entering the workforce, and tier-two and tier-three cities were growing enormously. All this put together provided headway for retail and consumer products.

The jewellery business was in a consolidation phase, after seismic changes in the taxation architecture with the introduction of the Goods and Services Tax (GST), the growth of the digital payments system post-demonetization and the government's BIS 916 initiative (referring to the finesse of gold jewellery, that is, 91.6 grams of gold per 100 grams). All of this accelerated a shift in consumer preference away from the highly fragmented unorganized sector and towards organized retail. Large-format retailers were now growing their market share in India.

Then, in the early weeks of 2020, came the greatest disruption the world economy had ever known.

The V-Shaped Recovery

Around the middle of February 2020, I was on a regular round of store visits, touring Singapore and Malaysia. On one of my flights, I noticed that every passenger on board was wearing a face mask, except me. I heard news of some sort of 'flu' doing the rounds and recalled that the media had reported a 'new virus' that was spreading rapidly. India's first case had been found in Kerala on 30 January 2020, when a university student from Wuhan had travelled back to the state. I didn't pay much attention, assuming that medical professionals would manage the upsurge of infections.

On my return to Dubai, I submerged myself in work. I travelled back to India on 9 March. Just two days later, on 11 March, the World Health Organization (WHO) declared the COVID-19 outbreak a pandemic. On 15 March, the Indian government imposed stringent travel restrictions; those coming from COVID-19 hot spots such as Italy, France, Spain and Iraq had to undergo mandatory quarantine.

As for me, by the time I got home, I had cough and cold. Jolly suggested that I move to a separate room, as I had all the symptoms of COVID-19. I didn't get myself tested, as very few labs were equipped to do so at the time. While I was recovering, India went into lockdown on 24 March 2020. Jolly, Elsa and I were confined to our home for the next two months, and we had a lot of fun together. As Jolly pointed out, that was the longest stretch of time I had spent with her after coming to Dubai! Elsa just happened to be with us, as she had finished her internship at the Taj Rambagh Palace Hotel in Jaipur, after graduating from Les Roches, Switzerland, in 2019.

I spent my time reading newspapers and watching television, mainly the news channels. There wasn't much else to do; all our stores, across eleven countries, had downed shutters. My only interaction with my team was over the telephone or on Zoom. We monitored the markets, of course; gold as an asset class reached an all-time high during the crisis.

The enforced isolation gave me time to plan for the future. For example, a few of my stores in the Gulf were not giving great returns on investment (ROI). My philosophy had been to keep the underperforming stores open, so as to ensure the brand's visibility in every part of the region. So, despite the low profits, the stores were allowed to continue. The COVID-induced disruption of business activity prompted me to reconsider the matter. I took the difficult decision to close down around a dozen stores. We then liquidated the inventory and brought down our bank debt to almost nil.

In India, things continued to look bleak, even after the lockdown had eased from July 2020. I was chafing at the enforced idleness, and decided to take a tour of all my stores in India. I hired a helicopter for the purpose and visited more than fifty stores, seeking to understand the business dynamics of each one. At the end of the trip, I was convinced of the urgent need for renovation/refurbishment (R/R) of the stores.

Renovation of outlets is an unavoidable part of the retail business. Every store undergoes R/R once every five years, to give it a new look and feel, and to incorporate the latest trends in interior fit-out and jewellery display. It usually takes two to three months, and the store is partially closed during this period. The disruption of normal functioning results in a significant loss of business. Thus, it is undertaken only when absolutely essential. Given the low customer footfall because of the pandemic, I decided to go in for a massive R/R exercise at most of our stores.

In the next three to five months, we completed the R/R of most of our stores. By the end of 2020, we were ready to welcome our customers. By this time, business activity had not only resumed, but surpassed pre-pandemic levels. There were multiple reasons for this. The first, of course, was that gold, as a safe haven asset, drew customers across all segments. The second was that of all the major economies, India's was the fastest growing, post-pandemic.

We benefitted from the renovation of our stores, because consumers preferred to shop in a sanitized space. Newly refurbished, our stores appeared clean and hygienic. They also offered a large retail space that allowed scope for social distancing. We had put in place robust sanitary measures and trained all our staff to assure customers of a safe retail experience.

Another big driver of demand was 'revenge spending'. The 'you only live once' (YOLO) mentality became pervasive post-pandemic, and encouraged spending, particularly on luxury goods like jewellery. The wedding segment, which accounts for approximately 50 per cent of the total demand in India, also drove sales. There were tight restrictions on the number of guests at wedding celebrations, with the result that the surplus in the wedding budget allowed more spending on jewellery.

The COVID-19 pandemic compelled us to look at every aspect of our business differently. For one thing, we made significant efforts towards cost reduction. This involved a minute examination of our operations to determine the optimum level of inventory and staff in each store and the kind of inventory in demand, as well as means of increasing the stock turnover, reducing power consumption and expediting renovation of our stores. It also enabled us to assess how much ought to be spent on advertisements and the price points to be negotiated with suppliers, bankers, landlords and so on.

I took note of even minor cost-cutting steps like setting the air-conditioning temperature controls at twenty-four degree Celsius rather than twenty-two, and replacing old bulbs with LEDs. The cumulative benefits of these small initiatives added to our performance. For me, the status quo was never acceptable; if there was a way to improve operational efficiency, or to save costs without undermining quality, we embraced it.

Our stringent cost-control measures translated into best-in-class margins. We also maintained our revenue in the financial year 2020–21, and despite two months of lockdown, we improved our margin significantly with a higher earnings before interest, taxes, depreciation, and amortization (EBITDA). I was the only jeweller who found a place in the Forbes' list of the 100 richest Indians in 2022. I must admit that I was quite chuffed!

Planning to Go Public ... Eventually

With our best-in-class industry margin thanks to our execution capabilities, better store economics, superior operating metrics, and long-standing track record of growth and profit, I can safely say that Joyalukkas is a sterling success story in the Indian jewellery sector.

The Indian predilection for jewellery and capacity to purchase it are an enigma for the rest of the world. As the exemplar of this industry, Joyalukkas offers an insight into Indian jewellery consumption and its growth story. So, I asked myself whether we ought to be a public-listed company to serve as a benchmark for the industry and lead the thrust towards excellence.

Going public involves shedding light on our operations and following stringent controls in ways not required of private companies. There's no doubt that in order to scale greater heights in the future, the business needs to build strong governance systems and financial controls. I have already embarked on that journey. We have moved to a robust enterprise resource planning (ERP) software, Microsoft Dynamics 365, and put in place internal committees for controls and processes. We are refining these systems as we go along.

Once these measures are in place, why should we not go public? I have never intended to be remain a private entity in perpetuity. My goal was always to build a sustainable company that could be publicly listed. In 2021, I decided with my head and heart to go in for a public listing.

Typically, it takes two to four years to become IPO-ready, depending on the company. Based on our previous experience with filing an IPO, we hope to be ready in the near future.

Our first step was to convert the private limited status of the company to a public one. That proved simple, but the decisions on expanding the board took some time. I didn't want my board to be stuffed with theoreticians, so I included entrepreneurs and company founders, who understood the language of business, and had boardroom and capital market experience. At the same time, I wanted someone with a strong background in finance to handle our audit and risk-management committees.

Accordingly, Alex K. Babu, founder of Hedge Equity, along with Lava Krishnan, managing director of SFS Homes, and finance professional Pushpy B. Muricken joined our board as independent directors. Alongside me, my son John Paul and our general manager of finance for international business, Thomas Scaria, also joined the board.

There is no perfect time for an IPO. You just keep the ball rolling, and launch when the IPO window is open. Not every company gets it right.

I have seen, and will be seeing, ups and downs in the market before we launch the IPO. My understanding of share prices is that markets don't always get it right in the short term, but they do get it right in the long term. I am going to leave some value on the table for investors, irrespective of the market pricing of my company.

12

Towards Glittering Tomorrows

On the afternoon of 8 September 2007, my four-seater Vulcanair P.68C turbo propeller aircraft took off from Bengaluru's HAL airport. The plane was en route to Kochi, to pick me up for a quick tour of Joyalukkas stores in Kerala and Tamil Nadu. As I waited, my phone rang; it was the airport control room informing me that the flight was delayed. Then, it rang for a second time. The call was from an unknown number, and it chilled me to the bone.

'Twin engine failure … two pilots … co-passengers … dead' came a breathless, panicky voice.

'Identify yourself and tell me what has happened,' I said, tersely.

My informant collected his wits and told me that he was a member of the ground crew, and had just received word that the aircraft had plunged into the Gowdanapalya lake to the south of Bengaluru city, killing all those on board.

In the horror of the moment, devastated by the tragic loss of life, my first thought was for the pilots' families. I made up my mind to pay them condolence visits as soon as possible.

On the following day, as I read the headline 'Plane crashes in Bangalore, 4 killed', I thought to myself, 'There, but for the grace of God, go I.' Whatever glitch had occurred could have taken place at any time. The plane may well have failed and gone into a fatal dive while I was on board. But fate had spared me.

People react to an awareness of mortality in different ways. The episode certainly gave me a renewed appreciation for the gift of life. Nor did I develop a fear of flying; a few years later, I bought another five-seater jet aircraft, and a few years after that, I upgraded to a seven-seater.

Most of all, it was a sort of call to arms. I had so much left to accomplish and a finite amount of time in which to do it. My determination to make Joyalukkas a global brand, sooner rather than later, deepened.

My life until that point had been a series of struggles. As a youth in Kerala, I was looked down upon by my older siblings, and my contributions to the family business were never acknowledged. Then, I landed in the Gulf, with no friends, no business contacts, no knowledge of the business ecosystem or the local language, and very little money. But I managed, through sheer determination and self-belief, to establish the Alukkas name in the UAE. After that came the family partition, which left me with no assets in my home country. In a matter of a few years, I leveraged my new-found freedom from family oversight to establish myself in India. I transitioned to a new identity while retaining the essence of the old.

From 2007 onwards, the business grew at an accelerated pace. As I write, we have 160 stores in eleven countries, and a turnover of three billion dollars, and we plan to grow in double digits year-on-year. Outside of the subcontinent and the Middle East, you can find Joyalukkas stores in the UK, the US, Singapore and Malaysia. Our money exchange business has grown and has ninety branches in the Gulf Cooperation Council countries. Today, we are poised for the next great leap forward.

In each phase of my life, I met with challenges that seemed insurmountable at the time. However, I have always had a tendency to go forward without thinking of the consequences. Had I bogged myself down in worrying about the potential ramifications of my decisions, I would most likely not have taken up those challenges. But I always managed to find an out-of-the-box solution. Often, I turned challenges into opportunities. I was able to accomplish all of this thanks in great measure to the learnings I had gained from my father: a never-say-die spirit, honesty in business dealings, empathy for all the stakeholders in my business, and a sharp eye on the bottom line.

Carpe Diem

I am often asked about my business philosophy. For me, success in business is about making the right choices. This calls for wisdom ('vivekam' in Malayalam); a combination of common sense, good judgment and a perspective shaped by experience. Wisdom is inborn, not learned. But it must be refined by observing others, listening to your instincts and honing your decision-making skills through trial and error.

Business acumen and sharpness of intellect alone do not suffice; one must seize opportunities and take advantage of them. For me, the UAE proved to be the land of opportunity. I am where I am today because fate brought me to Dubai, an environment in which I could use my innate skills to succeed. I found myself in perfect sync with its business culture, and grew along with the city. Today, I feel privileged to be able to say that Joyalukkas is the global face of Dubai's jewellery industry.

This doesn't mean sitting around and waiting for a lucky break. I don't believe in luck; rather, I believe that we make our own luck.

I have been blessed with sharp observational skills, a good memory and the ability to size up people. This makes me a good judge of character. Picking the right people to do business with or to hire is a valuable skill. As I always say, in Malayalam: 'Enikkavante khanam ariyam' (I know the weight of that person). So, I weigh the people I work with, and if I find a person competent and loyal, I repose my trust in him/her.

Staying ahead of the curve is strategically important. I always look to gain the first-mover advantage. Hanging back and waiting for someone else to test the waters first is not my style. If I believe in an idea, and I have calculated the odds, I go ahead. Being first and being different takes courage, and I attribute a large measure of my success to it.

Timing is crucial in terms of a new market entry. There's no point in being late to the table. If you miss the window of opportunity, you have lost out on the market.

One crucial piece of advice I received from my father, and have always followed rigorously, is to give primacy to the company's financial health. He used to say, 'Without finance, nonsense.' Be aware of margins and don't get confused by numbers. For example, if the cost of procuring a gold bangle is two dirhams and I sell it for four, that doesn't translate into a hundred per cent margin. Remember that if the cost of the gold itself is fifty dirhams, we sourced the bangle at fifty-two dirhams and sold it at fifty-four.

An important attribute for a businessman, to my mind, is humility. The moment you think you know it all, personal and professional progress ceases. Egocentrism leaves no space for creativity and personal growth. Be open to learning and ready to change. A flexible approach will take you much further, but a closed mind will keep you static.

I believe in carpe diem (seize the day). Learn how to live in the moment. Do not become a prisoner of the past or a hostage to the future. Who you are is rooted in the past; it shapes the way you think and act. But that cannot define your future. Be ready to move on, to abandon strategies that haven't worked, and never allow the 'sunk cost fallacy' to influence business decisions.

The strategies that brought you to a point may not work beyond it. So be ready to reinvent yourself, to constantly innovate and embrace change. This is particularly true of retail, one of the most dynamic and sensitive sectors in business. No retailer can afford to rest on his laurels, but many do, always to their detriment.

To cite another saying in Malayalam: 'Nikkunnidathu nikkanenki odikondirikkanam'. This can be broadly translated as, 'to remain where you are, you have to run'. Life is a treadmill; you have to keep running to stay in the same place.

In other words, if you want to go further, you have to spread your wings and fly.

The Simple Joys

My lifestyle is simple. I don't indulge in any extravagant idiosyncrasies to provide fodder for social media. All my spare time is spent with my family or people close to me, who are invariably 'work friends'.

On the face of it, this may sound like a dull lifestyle. But I find excitement in work, and contentment in being at home—chatting, cracking jokes and even pulling pranks on my family and friends. When someone asks me what I do for fun, I am always a bit stumped. 'Fun' is a relative concept. Watching sports is fun; I love football, so I went to Qatar to see a couple of matches during the 2022 World Cup. The most fun I have, however, is at work.

There's always a thrill in finding the perfect location for a new store or planning a unique product launch. And there's nothing more soothing than the laughter and banter between family members while cooking. I like to cook; my signature dish is a Kerala-style fish curry, the kind my mother used to make. The wholesome Kerala fare is far more to my taste than exotic cuisines. A combination of hard work and a frugal diet have kept me fit and energetic. I remain reasonably trim, which is a blessing.

I travel a lot, invariably for work. John Paul often points out that I don't 'see' anything on my trips overseas. He is right; I have no interest in conventional tourism. I go from the airport to my hotel and from there, to the store or the office. I choose my hotels for cleanliness and convenience, not for luxury. My initial years in the UAE, of living in hotels and travelling rough, have inured me to minor discomforts. So, I don't care how many stars a hotel has, or whether a restaurant has a Michelin rating.

Jolly is my mainstay. She has always supported me unconditionally and kept me grounded, while giving me enough space to do whatever I wanted to in terms of business. I'm not the easiest person to live with; I know that and give her full credit for her having adjusted to my quirks. She is a deeply moral person. It is to her and to my father that I owe my own moral compass.

For the last decade, Jolly has spent more time at our home in Thrissur than in Dubai. I had nurtured the ambition of having a home of my own in India for so long that I decided to go all out. Every aspect of the Joy Alukkas mansion in Thrissur has been built according to my specifications, and has become something of a landmark in the city.

When Elsa enrolled in a psychology programme at a college in Thrissur in 2012, Jolly decided to move to India with her. By that time, Mary was married to Antony Jos Chirakkekkaran and John Paul to Sonia George Mundackal. It was not an easy transition, as Jolly had been in the UAE since 1987. Her life was in Dubai. Deeply religious, she was a lay minister at St. Mary's Church in Dubai, which has the largest parish in the world.

With characteristic resilience, she adjusted to Thrissur and involved herself in church activities. She also holds a weekly prayer meeting with my sisters and other members of both our families. She's quite close to her sisters-in-law, and they often undertake charity work together. Every morning, she picks up a friend or two and goes to church, after which they have breakfast together. Like my parents, she never misses mass.

Our family has grown, now that all three of the children are married. Mary's husband, Antony Jos, heads our money exchange business; while Elsa's husband Thomas Mathew is a techie at Apple Inc. and is based in the US. I hope to see him join our Indian operations in the future.

We have six grandchildren, the oldest of whom is Michelle. She is followed, in chronological order, by Thea, Hazel, Julia, Lionel Joy and Jos. Note that the youngest of John Paul's three children is called Lionel Joy after the football legend Messi, because my son shares my passion for the game! I love all my grandchildren equally, although the first one is always special. I am not the classic doting grandfather, because I have never been given to overt expressions of love towards children. My own children will attest to that. But they are the centre of my universe, and they know it.

Philanthropy, the Right Way

Jolly and I believe in effective philanthropy. For us, 'giving back' is a moral duty, and part of that duty is making sure that the funds actually make a difference to society. This calls for carefully assessing which projects to fund, clearly laying out the deliverables and monitoring the outcomes.

To that end, Jolly and I set up The Joyalukkas Foundation, dedicated to improving the lives of the most underprivileged in the world. Jolly heads the foundation and I can think of no one better suited to the task. My wife is a deeply spiritual and generous individual, who has managed to inspire and imbue our whole team with her compassionate spirit.

The foundation has been providing financial aid for education, medical treatments, disaster relief and construction of homes, and is now looking to expand and align its range of activities with Sustainable Development Goals. Today, environmental, social and corporate governance (ESG) agendas are transforming businesses, and are increasingly driving consumer choices.

In 'greening' Joyalukkas, we plan to introduce eco-friendly packaging, while raising environmental awareness among our customers by sharing eco-friendly tips with them. Ensuring that supply chains are ethical is integral to the ESG framework. To that end, we are orienting ourselves towards responsible purchasing/sourcing, while educating our customers on fair business practices.

We are also introducing an in-house volunteering programme. Joyalukkas employees will be encouraged to participate in our CSR activities, with each committing a certain number of hours. In order to demonstrate to our customers that we are making efforts towards environmental and social responsibility, we hope to obtain the requisite certification. We are also looking to participate in global 'green' and social initiatives by partnering with international entities and government authorities.

Among other initiatives, we want to promote digital inclusion. The COVID-19 pandemic underlined the urgent need to bridge the digital divide in India. A majority of children from low-income rural households were unable to access information and communication technologies and fell behind in their education. On the health front, the rising incidences of cancer has prompted us to fund a research centre for cancer. All these plans are already in motion, and are aligned with my father's philanthropic endeavours.

The Future: A Joyride

In my lifetime, the jewellery retail business has undergone tectonic changes. From standalone stores to organized retail chains to e-commerce platforms, distribution and marketing channels and consumption patterns have altered beyond recognition. Technology is the greatest disruptor and driver of change. Companies around the world are preparing for the brave new 'metaverse', and Joyalukkas intends to build its own brand experiences in that space. That's just one of the many challenges ahead.

Going forward, we are looking at restructuring the company to bring it more in sync with current trends in corporate governance. For example, from 2000 onwards, we have followed a circular organizational structure, broadly shaped like concentric circles with me in the centre. This format imparted the agility that was needed at the time.

We had a workforce of around five hundred across the GCC, distributed over various departments. The departmental heads reported directly to me, an absolute necessity as many of them needed hand-holding, and several of the issues that arose demanded personal intervention on my part. This structure worked very well for a couple of decades and allowed us to achieve all our milestones. I had absolute control over each and every aspect of the business, and all the managers had direct access to me.

With the growth of the company, we now feel the need to transition to a scalar organizational structure, with a clearly delineated chain of authority from the highest level of management to the lowest. In this model, responsibility flows in a vertical line from top to bottom, one rung at a time.

The restructuring process is currently underway. I am referring, of course, to the jewellery retail business, which accounts for a substantial part of our turnover. This comprises two entities: Joyalukkas India Ltd and Joyalukkas Holdings Inc. The money exchange and other divisions function as separate verticals.

As a family-owned business, we tend to be more flexible than corporate entities, which enables us to evolve and adjust to the changing priorities and needs of our stakeholders. In addition, we have a constant influx of talent as new generations of the family join the business, bringing their skills with them. However, simultaneously running and owning a business raises the question of accountability.

Increasingly, family businesses are looking to institutionalize accountability. It is important to have external independent directors on the company board who can hold the management to account. Our board now has three independent directors. We are also setting up advisory councils to provide oversight and guidance on the strategic direction of the company.

As we restructure, we are moving towards a combined decision-making framework, involving committees at various levels. We are in the process of drawing up standard operating procedures (SOPs), policies and manuals to assist the senior management team in taking decisions. The SOPs will give relevant authority along with responsibility and ownership.

Investing in People

I see myself as a people person, and I believe that the ability to bring out the best in them is the hallmark of effective leadership.

Finding and nurturing talent is essential to the success of any company. One of the reasons for moving our corporate office from Thrissur to a metropolis—Bengaluru—is to facilitate access to the best and brightest India has to offer.

Of late, I have been attempting to increase the number of women employees at Joyalukkas. A few years ago, we hired six young women for our India operations, and I have been deeply impressed by their dynamism and dedication. They have exceptional sales skills and can handle any assignment. I intend to promote women as assistant managers and managers at our stores. I also envisage senior positions for women at our corporate office, particularly in HR and marketing.

In the next five years, 30 per cent of all the positions in our Indian company will be filled by women. This is not just in keeping with the times, but is a very practical move. It widens our talent pool, and this in turn, contributes to the growth and success of the company.

For me, grassroots-level employee involvement is vital. I have always engaged with people at the bottom of the company pyramid. My open-door policy allowed just about anyone to come and see me. Now, as we move towards a more hierarchical structure, I want to ensure a free flow of information, so that every employee is not only heard but receives feedback. I regard the 9,000-odd employees of Joyalukkas as part of an extended family. Every worker must feel relevant and have a sense of ownership and pride in the company. Additionally, a lack of communication can result in important issues being ignored.

I strongly believe that investing in people pays off many times over. The role of friendship, founded on mutual trust and confidence, in my success cannot be underrated. Chemmanur George Varghese, Jassim Al Hasawi, Yusuf Nunu—all of them took a chance on me. Varghese gave me a guarantee—no questions asked and no collateral—that enabled me to open my first store. Al Hasawi supported me through my struggles during the early years. Nunu provided me with the means to set up a retail chain, the first of its kind in the GCC. They believed in me. And for that, I will be eternally grateful to them.

Rejuvenating Brand Joyalukkas

Maintaining brand equity means staying authentic to your core values, even as you grow. After successfully negotiating rebranding, a global financial crisis and a global pandemic, the brand remains strong—a testimony to our ceaseless commitment to our customers and our capacity for reinvention.

Recognizing that Industry 4.0 is profoundly impacting modes of doing business, we are crafting a new-age business identity. We are looking at an omnichannel retail model that will offer customers a seamless shopping experience, as well as new e-commerce brands and growth engines such as product lines in 18-karat jewellery.

Expanding the Joyalukkas footprint will also be realized through the franchise model. We envisage a network of franchisees across the globe, offering the superior quality, purity, designs and customer experience that have become synonymous with Joyalukkas.

In the process of becoming future-ready, I continue to provide hands-on leadership. John Paul and my sons-in-law are doing well in their respective professional roles, but no one has so far emerged as the heir apparent. In business, everybody has to prove their calibre, and my family members are no exception.

The Joyalukkas legacy, built over the last three-and-a-half decades, will pass into the hands of a successor who has the capacity to meet the immense challenges of the future and ensure the longevity of the brand. I am in my late sixties and quite fit for my age, so there's time enough for potential successors to mature and consolidate their experiences and positions.

Ever since my mid-fifties, I have been asked, 'So, when are you planning to retire?' I used to say that I would lay down the mantle when I turned sixty. That milestone came and went; I barely noticed its passing, so involved was I in the growth of the business. I began to say that I would quit at sixty-five, and I actually believed it. But that birthday, too, has passed and I still feel that much, much more remains to be done.

For me, work has become more exciting, not less. It stimulates me, and lends a vibrancy to my life. By the infinite grace of God, I have the energy, the drive and the desire to keep soldiering on. The anticipation of an action-packed day at work gets me out of bed in the morning. I haven't tired of the world of business, and it hasn't tired of me.

My retirement stands postponed, indefinitely.

A Note from the Coauthors

For us, the coauthors of the Joy Alukkas story, the man is little short of a living legend.

So, it was with trepidation that we took up the challenge of capturing his life in a book. What would we discover about him in the process? Were there traumas, beliefs or intimate stories that he had kept to himself all these years? How far should we burrow into his past?

For eighteen months, we delved into every aspect of his life, personal and professional. We conducted over 6,000 minutes of interviews with Joy alone and spoke with more than a hundred of his relatives, friends, adversaries, competitors and co-workers.

What emerged from our research was a leader with a rare combination of genius and passion. Behind a quiet and unassuming exterior lay a ferocious drive to succeed—one that recognized no boundaries, limits or accepted norms.

That implacable will didn't just establish the largest family-run jewellery chain in the world, it revolutionized the jewellery industry itself.

What makes his success so incredible is the fact that he overcame apparently insurmountable odds. A big part of his personal and professional success is owed to his ability to put his faith in people who have the confidence and passion to execute their tasks. He has given them a platform and unfettered freedom, regardless of their education or past performance. For instance, when we presented the idea of this book, he didn't question our thinking or our lack of experience!

Like us, he has enabled hundreds to grow to their full potential. Every person we interviewed cherishes that one special moment with him, regardless of where they are now or how their relationship has evolved over time.

One aspect that struck us forcefully is his hunger to learn. It's part of his internal makeup. He constantly asks questions, for example, about the status of projects. He is inventive, imaginative and bold in his reasoning, with the result that he has come up with pioneering initiatives that have made him a veritable torchbearer of the jewellery industry. An artful combination of traditional and cutting-edge business practices has given Joyalukkas an undeniable edge.

He manages to challenge his team without instilling in them a fear of failure, often to excellent effect. When it comes to decision-making, he tends not to over-analyse or procrastinate.

His default demeanour is calm, soft-spoken and unassuming, but he masks a fierce determination and tenacity. Patience and perseverance are his defining virtues; he has the ability to pursue a goal relentlessly until it has been achieved.

He considers two conflicting ideas, thereby becoming his own devil's advocate. In business, he does not follow the herd or subscribe to established axioms. He reflexively attunes himself to market changes. He has the ability to simultaneously look at the big picture and assess granular details, which has proved invaluable in his success.

His unconventional thinking, intuition and imagination make him hard to decipher. Such is his drive that he can whip up people into a frenzy. Conversely, he can calm them down with his good sense.

As a leader, he is not given to motivational speeches or excessive handholding. He prefers to give his people room to grow, even if that means making mistakes. In fact, he seldom castigates employees for their failures, and has been known to overlook grave errors that led to adverse consequences, provided he believed the mistake was unintentional. Similarly, he expects people around him to be nonjudgmental with regard to his own lapses.

His life story is instructive, in that it holds lessons on leadership and its attributes, such as character, values, vision, self-awareness and strategic thinking.

'Joy Sir', as we fondly refer to him, cooperated fully in the writing of this book, and gave us total creative freedom. Nothing was off-limits. He encouraged everyone who contributed to speak honestly. He was himself remarkably candid. His family, friends, foes and colleagues together gave us an unexpurgated view of the passion, perfectionism and artistry that shaped his approach to business and resulted in the creation of the brand Joyalukkas.

We have done our best to do justice to his story and portray the extraordinary life of an extraordinary man.

Acknowledgements

Anyone who's written a book will tell you what a difficult exercise it is, and they are absolutely right. Building a business is a challenge, but writing comes a close second. I am fortunate to have had the support of a bunch of fine people, who helped me bring it to fruition. I could not have done it without them.

First and foremost, I must thank my wife, Jolly, the continuous thread in the story of my life.

I couldn't have asked for better collaborators than my coauthors, Thomas Scaria and Nidhi Jain, who came up with excellent story ideation and narration. They spent many hours each day organizing and structuring the material.

Somyah Gupta served as an adviser and planned the project. Diana Varghese translated and transcribed the interviews. Bhavdeep Kang and Namita Kala helped me edit the manuscript.

I also thank the people featured in the book for sharing their stories, research and ideas. I must also acknowledge all those who helped me find my feet in Dubai, and the great city itself, for the inclusive spirit that enabled a young man to realize his dreams. And last but not least, Sachin Sharma of HarperCollins Publishers India, who was always available to render much-needed advice.

Index

About the Author

Joy Alukkas is the founder and chairman of the eponymous global retail brand Joyalukkas Jewellery. Originally from Thrissur in Kerala, he is credited with modernizing the Indian jewellery retail business globally. Branching out on his own from a family-run business, he disrupted the traditional model of standalone jewellery stores and created a global chain comprising 160 stores in India, the Middle East, Southeast Asia, the UK and the US. His diverse business interests include forex remittance and textile retail under the brand name Joyalukkas Exchange and Jolly Silks, respectively. He figures on the Forbes' Billionaires list of 2023 and is regarded as one of the most prominent business leaders of the Arab world.

About the Coauthors

Thomas Scaria is a Fellow Chartered Accountant of India and the UK with over two decades of experience in financial strategies. Currently the General Manager (Finance) of Joyalukkas International and a member of its board of directors in India, he has worked closely with Joy Alukkas and learnt from him, gaining intimate insights into his professional and personal life. Having grown with the company in different roles, he has led various projects in acquisition, debt and equity financing. He is an avid reader of nonfiction books and has a great passion for teaching.

Nidhi Jain is a writer, broadcaster, TV producer and media consultant. A journalist by training, she graduated from the Indian Institute of Mass Communication and worked with All India Radio, TV Today's Aaj Tak news channel and Sony Entertainment Television in India before moving to Dubai as a programme director with TEN Sports. She also served as a relationship manager with the Emirates NBD Bank, Dubai. She has a deep interest in finance and psychology.

HarperCollins *Publishers* India

At HarperCollins India, we believe in telling the best stories and finding the widest readership for our books in every format possible. We started publishing in 1992; a great deal has changed since then, but what has remained constant is the passion with which our authors write their books, the love with which readers receive them, and the sheer joy and excitement that we as publishers feel in being a part of the publishing process.

Over the years, we've had the pleasure of publishing some of the finest writing from the subcontinent and around the world, including several award-winning titles and some of the biggest bestsellers in India's publishing history. But nothing has meant more to us than the fact that millions of people have read the books we published, and that somewhere, a book of ours might have made a difference.

As we look to the future, we go back to that one word— a word which has been a driving force for us all these years.

Read.

Harper
Collins

HARPER
PERENNIAL

HARPER
BUSINESS

HARPER
BLACK

हार्पर
हिन्दी

HarperCollins
Children'sBooks

HARPER
DESIGN

HARPER
VANTAGE

Harper
Sport